PURSUIT OF AN IDENTITY

Finding Your True Self on the Entrepreneurial Journey

RAJ GOPAL

STARDOM BOOKS

www.StardomBooks.com

STARDOM BOOKS
112 Bordeaux Ct.
Coppell, TX 75019, USA

Copyright © 2025 by RAJ GOPAL

All rights reserved. No part of this book may be reproduced or used in any manner without written permission of the copyright owner except for the use of quotations in a book review.

FIRST EDITION JANUARY 2025

STARDOM BOOKS, LLC.
112 Bordeaux Ct. Coppell, TX 75019, USA

www.stardombooks.com

Stardom Books, United States
Stardom Alliance, India

The author and publishers have made all reasonable efforts to contact copyright holders for permission and apologize for any omissions or errors in the form of credits given. Corrections may be made to future editions.

PURSUIT OF AN IDENTITY
Finding Your True Self on the Entrepreneurial Journey

RAJ GOPAL

p. 142
cm. 13.97 X 21.59

Category:
BUSINESS & ECONOMICS/Entrepreneurship
SELF-HELP/Personal Growth/Success
SELF-HELP/Motivational & Inspirational

ISBN: 978-1-957456-62-1

To my parents, to whom I am forever indebted.
To my wife Ragini and son Aditya, who are my greatest support.
And to all the aspiring entrepreneurs striving to make up their minds.

CONTENTS

	ACKNOWLEDGMENTS	*i*
	PREFACE	1
	INTRODUCTION	3
Ch. 1.	BREAKING THE CHAINS OF FEAR	5
Ch. 2.	CRAFTING YOUR ENTREPRENEURIAL VISION	21
Ch. 3.	CULTIVATING DISCIPLINE AND RESILIENCE	47
Ch. 4.	UNDERSTANDING YOUR UNIQUE VALUE PROPOSITION	69
Ch. 5.	BUILDING YOUR NICHE AND MARKET STRATEGY	89
Ch. 6.	DELIVERING EXCEPTIONAL VALUE TO CUSTOMERS	103
	CONCLUSION	131

ACKNOWLEDGMENTS

To the entire Fidrox team for their unwavering support, and especially to S. Krushna Kumar, without whose encouragement I might never have made the decision to become an entrepreneur.

To all my ex-colleagues, partners, and professionals I have worked with, who have been invaluable in shaping my learning and contributing to my personal and professional growth.

To all my teachers and professors, whose guidance and wisdom have contributed to my learning and to whom I am forever grateful.

To the entire Stardom team, and to Raam Anand, who convinced and inspired me to embark on this writing journey, as well as the dedicated team of Ranjitha Vijayakumar, Sanjana Ghosh, Aakruti Ramakrishnan, Rekha Krishnaprasad, and Chaya Shetty who supported the entire process.

PREFACE

As I embarked on my entrepreneurial journey many years ago, I had little idea that the path ahead would be about much more than business. I thought I was setting out to create a company, build a product/solution, and achieve financial success. But what I didn't anticipate was how this journey would lead me on a deeper quest—one that went far beyond profits and growth metrics. It became a journey of self-discovery, a pursuit of my own identity.

Entrepreneurship is often portrayed as a heroic tale of hustle, innovation, and risk-taking. But beneath the surface of these common narratives lies something much more personal: the story of how we, as entrepreneurs, struggle to find who we truly are. We grapple with fear, face failure, question our worth, and constantly evolve, not only as business owners but as individuals. I realized early on that entrepreneurship isn't just about what you build but about who you become in the process.

This book, Pursuit of an Identity, is the culmination of years of introspection and experience, both my own and those of countless entrepreneurs I've had the privilege of working with. It reflects the challenges, triumphs, and revelations that come when you choose to align your business goals with your true self.

Through this book, I want to take you on a similar journey—one that will help you reflect on who you are, what you value, and how your entrepreneurial pursuits can serve as a mirror to your own growth and transformation. My hope is that by the end of this book, you will not only have the tools to succeed in business but also the clarity to embrace your identity along the way.

The entrepreneurial journey can be a lonely one. The challenges we face often feel personal, as if no one else can quite understand the internal battles we wage. But I want to assure you that you are not alone. The struggle for identity is one that many of us face, and it is a struggle worth engaging in because the rewards go far beyond any external measure of success. They touch the core of who we are.

As you read through the pages of this book, I encourage you to reflect on your own journey. Think about the fears you've faced, the vision you hold for your life, and the discipline you've cultivated to pursue it. My hope is that the stories, insights, and strategies shared in this book will help you navigate the challenges of entrepreneurship while staying true to the most important asset you possess—yourself.

So, welcome to the journey. This is not just a book about business; it's a book about becoming. Let's begin.

INTRODUCTION

In Pursuit of an Identity is a book born from a question I have grappled with throughout my entrepreneurial journey: *Who am I, and what does my work say about me?* While many of us are drawn to entrepreneurship to create something meaningful, our paths often reveal challenges we didn't anticipate—not just in business but within ourselves. This journey uncovers a deeper search, one that asks us to confront our fears, discover our purpose, and, ultimately, find our identity.

As entrepreneurs, we are often preoccupied with tangible outcomes: launching products, meeting targets, growing our businesses. But I believe there's an equally vital, often overlooked outcome—our personal transformation. The process of building a business, with all its trials and triumphs, becomes a mirror reflecting back who we truly are. Through our setbacks, resilience, visions, and growth, we embark on an inward journey as much as an outward one.

This book is meant to be your guide on that journey. Throughout these pages, I invite you to explore not just the practical aspects of entrepreneurship but also the personal insights that come with it. Together, we'll address the fears that hold you back, the vision that drives you forward, and the resilience that keeps you going. We'll uncover your unique value proposition, helping you build a business that isn't only successful but deeply aligned with who you are.

This journey is for those who seek to create not only a thriving business but a meaningful life. You may be looking to make an impact, build something greater than yourself, or simply find clarity in your path. Whatever your motivation, I believe that this pursuit—of identity, purpose, and alignment—is the most important journey you can undertake as an entrepreneur.

Let's embark on this path together, starting with the first step: recognizing and embracing who you are.

Chapter 1
BREAKING THE CHAINS OF FEAR

"Everything you want is on the other side of fear."

— Jack Canfield

Imagine standing at the edge of a cliff, your heart pounding, your palms sweaty. Below you is the unknown, a leap into entrepreneurship that feels as daunting as this physical abyss. Now, imagine taking that leap and discovering you have wings. This chapter is about finding those wings, breaking the chains of fear that hold you back, and soaring into the realm of entrepreneurship.

Fear, the single most significant barrier to entrepreneurship, can be transformed. It's not the lack of resources, connections, or time that holds most people back, but their fears. In this chapter, we will explore the nature of these fears, their potency, and how understanding and overcoming them can be a catalyst for transformation, not just for your business but also for your personal growth.

And I don't say this lightly. It comes from a place of experience and sight that even I have had to harbor over years and years. I was also in your shoes once, 25 years ago, standing on the precipice of starting my own venture. But I took that leap, faced my fears, and discovered my wings. This chapter is about finding your wings, breaking the chains of fear that hold you back, and soaring into entrepreneurship.

Fear is an inevitable phenomenon for entrepreneurs, but it can be either a deterrent or a motivator. It can influence motivation, decision-making, and behavior in both positive and negative ways. Fear can push entrepreneurs to work harder but can also contribute to increased stress and worse health outcomes.

But what exactly is fear?

Entrepreneurs often grapple with fear at some point in their journey. It's like this invisible force that lurks in the background, making us hesitant to take risks or chase after our dreams. Sometimes, it's the very thing that stops us from diving into entrepreneurship altogether. But here's the twist: fear can also be the kick in the pants that propels entrepreneurs toward greatness.

Fear is a natural reaction to the risky and the unknown. In the business realm, it comes in many forms - fear of failure, rejection, the unknown, or even success itself. It can paralyze us, but it can also light a fire under us. Fear keeps us sharp, pushing us to work harder and smarter. For some, a healthy fear of failure keeps them on their toes, always striving to do better. In fact, fear can sometimes be the secret sauce that turns a good entrepreneur into a great one. So, let's not shy away from fear; let's harness it as a powerful motivator on our journey to greatness.

Many of my colleagues, and perhaps even I, didn't initially have a mindset to become entrepreneurs. I was content being an employee elsewhere. It took some effort, and I believe most of us are so operationally involved that we rarely think beyond our daily tasks. Often, these offbeat thoughts about pursuing something different get pushed aside due to our constant engagement in our work.

Especially as a businessperson, you're constantly preoccupied with something or the other. That is the noise factor we must rise above. I've observed several talented colleagues who could potentially initiate their entrepreneurial ventures but have refrained from doing so because they have well-paying jobs and are reluctant to take risks. Since I took the plunge, many of them have approached me to discuss the possibility of venturing out on their own. However, many are still hesitant, which is a common concern, particularly among first-time entrepreneurs from a middle-class background, regarding the fear of failure and uncertainty about success.

I've closely observed several entrepreneurs, particularly some of my former colleagues, who are undeniably talented but often focus excessively on the technical aspects of their products or solutions without adequately validating them with customers. While they may occasionally have well-thought-out offerings, their positioning or ability to connect with customers tends to be lacking. There's a common misconception that a good product alone is enough to drive sales. However, in today's fast-paced world, gaining access to clients and effectively communicating the benefits of your product can take time and effort. It's crucial to conduct research to understand the customer's current situation and demonstrate how your offering can positively impact them.

Many of these entrepreneurs prioritize technical aspects over marketing communication or customer validation. It's essential to engage in consultation with potential clients to identify problems and develop solutions that address their needs. This approach not only helps create a market footprint but also guides your overall strategy. Depending on the nature of your offering, especially in a B2B context, consulting with businesses to develop solutions with clear business cases is vital. Once you've created something valuable and affordable, clients are likely to adopt it, allowing you to iterate and expand your client base. This strategic focus on customer validation and marketing communication can be a game-changer in your entrepreneurial journey.

Planning is paramount in entrepreneurship, providing a sense of security and preparedness. It encompasses everything from understanding the customer to developing solutions and assembling teams. Building a trustworthy team that is open to challenges and eager to contribute is crucial. Success as an entrepreneur, particularly in B2B ventures, requires a well-rounded approach that considers various aspects of business and solution development.

For many newcomers in the entrepreneurial world, fear of failure is the giant monster under the bed. And let's be honest, failing in business can sting - financially, emotionally, you name it. But here's an empowering concept - 'fail fast.' The idea is to embrace failure as part of the process, learn from it, and move on quickly. It's about taking calculated risks, not diving headfirst without a plan. This approach can be a source of encouragement, pushing us to take the necessary risks to make our ventures soar.

Fear, in an entrepreneurial set-up, generally manifests and mainly revolves around the challenges of comprehensively planning a business. Most individuals come from a single stream of work, such as technical, sales, or finance, and may need more familiarity with a holistic approach to business planning. This can lead to concerns about forming a team or overlooking crucial aspects of the business. There's always an element of uncertainty, where success can make you feel accomplished, while failure may leave you feeling like you've missed something crucial. Personally, more than the fear of being an entrepreneur, my hesitation stemmed from not having planned for it. I was content with my corporate life until I grew bored with its monotony, the usual Monday to Friday calls, and no challenges coming my way, especially in a role lacking creativity and significant solutions. With my extensive industry experience, including managing P&Ls and establishing new business territories, I felt equipped to embark on my own venture. Planning became critical; identifying opportunities, assembling a team, and even reaching out to potential customers beforehand were key steps. Only when everything was in place did I decide to take the leap; I believe planning directly correlates with an enterprise's success potential.

One other common reason why many people hesitate to pursue entrepreneurship is the challenge of funding. So naturally, it's crucial to break down why you need those funds and what you plan to do with them. Whether in a startup or an established organization, constraints are always present. While larger companies may have certain resources readily available, they still operate under their own set of constraints.

In the case of startups, the primary constraint often revolves around limited access to funds and resources. In my own experience, funding was a concern when we started our venture. We had to strategically plan around this limitation and actively seek ways to secure funding, which involved working with banks and other financial institutions to secure overdraft facilities.

Maintaining credibility is essential in this process. It's crucial to deliver on promises and demonstrate seriousness and commitment. Fortunately, there are various avenues for accessing funds today, including banks, seed capital, venture capitalists, and other funding stages. However, the challenge lies in choosing the right funding source and managing the fear of potential loss associated with it.

Moreover, familial support can be a significant factor. In many cases, family members may be hesitant to support entrepreneurial endeavors due to the perceived risks involved. This lack of support can further amplify the challenges associated with funding. In my own case, I faced similar hurdles, keeping my venture a secret from my family for the initial years until it proved successful. Only then did I reveal my entrepreneurial pursuits, as I knew they would be more supportive once they saw tangible results.

Consider the giants of entrepreneurship—Walt Disney, Steve Jobs, and Oprah Winfrey. They all experienced setbacks before they achieved greatness. If you're not aware of what they faced, let me enlighten you.

Walt Disney's journey to success was fraught with numerous challenges. In the early 1920s, Disney founded his first animation studio, Laugh-O-Gram Studio, in Kansas City. Despite facing financial difficulties and eventually going bankrupt, he never gave up on his dream.

Undeterred, Disney moved to Hollywood in 1923 to pursue his passion for animation. Alongside his brother Roy, he established the Disney Brothers Studio, which later became The Walt Disney Company. Despite early successes with the creation of Oswald the

Lucky Rabbit cartoons, Disney lost the rights to the character due to a contractual dispute with his distributor.

Determined to rebound from this setback, Disney and his team created Mickey Mouse, who made his debut in the groundbreaking animated short film "Steamboat Willie" in 1928. Mickey Mouse became an instant sensation and catapulted Disney to fame and success. However, Disney's challenges were far from over.

Throughout the 1930s and 1940s, Disney faced financial difficulties, labor strikes, and the challenges of producing feature-length animated films such as 'Snow White and the Seven Dwarfs' and 'Fantasia.' Despite these obstacles, Disney's creativity, innovation, and unwavering commitment to quality carved the path for the establishment of Disneyland in 1955 and the expansion of The Walt Disney Company into a global entertainment empire. One of the key strategies Disney employed was to always prioritize quality over quantity, a principle that still guides the company today.

Then we have Steve Jobs. Jobs' entrepreneurial journey was a rollercoaster of triumphs and tribulations, showcasing his remarkable resilience. In 1976, Jobs co-founded Apple Computer Inc. in his parents' garage with Steve Wozniak and Ronald Wayne. Despite internal conflicts and power struggles, he remained steadfast in his pursuit of success. One of the key factors that contributed to his success was his ability to envision and create products that revolutionized the technology industry, such as the Macintosh, iPod, and iPhone.

In 1985, Jobs was ousted from Apple following a contentious dispute with then-CEO John Sculley. Undeterred, Jobs went on to found NeXT Computer Inc., a computer hardware and software company. Despite producing innovative products, including the NeXTcube workstation, NeXT struggled to gain significant market share. However, the lessons Jobs learned from this failure, such as the importance of market research and understanding customer needs, would later prove instrumental in his success with Apple.

In 1986, Jobs acquired Pixar Animation Studios from Lucasfilm's computer graphics division. Pixar initially faced financial difficulties and struggled to find success with its early films. However, the release of "Toy Story" in 1995 marked a turning point for the company, establishing Pixar as a powerhouse in the animation industry.

Jobs returned to Apple in 1997 when the company acquired NeXT. As interim CEO, he orchestrated a remarkable turnaround, introducing groundbreaking products such as the iMac, iPod, iPhone, and iPad. Under Jobs' leadership, Apple became one of the most valuable and influential technology companies in the world, revolutionizing the way we communicate, work, and live. His vision and relentless pursuit of excellence continue to shape the tech industry to this day, with Apple's products setting new standards for design, functionality, and user experience.

Oprah Winfrey's journey from a difficult childhood to a media mogul is a testament to her resilience and determination in the face of adversity. Born into poverty in rural Mississippi, Winfrey endured a problematic upbringing marked by poverty, abuse, and instability. Despite these challenges, she excelled academically and began her broadcasting career while still in high school, a time when opportunities for African American women in the media industry were scarce and discrimination was rampant.

In 1976, Winfrey moved to Baltimore to co-anchor the evening news. However, her unorthodox style and emotional approach to storytelling led to her dismissal. Undeterred, Winfrey relocated to Chicago, where she hosted a morning talk show, "AM Chicago." The show's success led to a national syndication deal, and in 1986, it was renamed "The Oprah Winfrey Show."

Despite facing skepticism and discrimination as an African American woman in the media industry, Winfrey's authenticity, empathy, and ability to connect with her audience propelled her to unprecedented success. Her genuine interest in people's stories and her ability to make them feel seen and heard were the key to her show's success. 'The Oprah Winfrey Show' became the highest-rated talk show in television history, reaching millions of viewers worldwide.

In addition to her talk show, Winfrey established Harpo Productions, a multimedia production company responsible for producing films, television shows, and magazines. She also launched the Oprah Winfrey Network (OWN), a cable television channel dedicated to inspirational programming.

Throughout her career, Winfrey has used her platform to advocate for social justice, education, and empowerment, earning her numerous accolades and honors, including the Presidential Medal of Freedom.

These three entrepreneurs' stories are not just tales of success, but they are also powerful narratives of perseverance. They remind us that success often requires overcoming significant obstacles and setbacks. Their unwavering determination, creativity, and resilience continue to inspire generations of aspiring entrepreneurs around the world.

But here's the real lesson: they didn't allow failure to define them. Instead, they used it as a transformative tool on their path to success. Their journeys should serve as a potent reminder that failure is merely a temporary obstacle, a stepping stone on the path to success.

Adopting and nurturing a positive mindset can be a game-changer when it comes to conquering the fear of failure. Successful entrepreneurs recognize that failure is part of the journey, but it doesn't have to be the destination. They view challenges as opportunities to learn and thrive. By reframing our perception of failure, we can concentrate on the victories and the lessons learned along the way rather than dwelling on the failures. This optimistic perspective can ignite our determination and guide us toward success.

So, fear doesn't have to be our kryptonite. It can be the push we need to reach our goals. The key is understanding its role, taking risks when needed, and keeping our eyes on the prize. Fear should never stop us from chasing our dreams; it should fuel our determination to make them a reality.

Validate assumptions with potential customers and understand their current experiences and pain points. Tailor the communication and positioning of the offering to highlight the benefits and advantages for the customer, ensuring they feel understood and catered to. Consult with potential clients during the solution development process to ensure it addresses a real problem and has a strong business case. Build a team with diverse expertise and foster trust and collaboration among team members. Adopt a well-rounded approach that considers various aspects, including planning, marketing, communication, and team building. Plan comprehensively, covering all aspects of the endeavor. Identify opportunities and develop solutions. Involve relevant stakeholders, including support functions, technical teams, and customer-facing personnel. Assign responsibilities and ensure accountability. Take the initiative to engage stakeholders, build confidence, and drive execution. Recognize the role of luck in achieving success.

To sum it up, I'd emphasize the importance of planning. The plan should encompass all aspects, taking a holistic approach. It should outline what you intend to offer, identify opportunities, and detail how you plan to deliver solutions. It would be best if you considered everyone involved, from support functions to technical and customer-facing roles. Planning requires envisioning the people needed, conversing with them, and inspiring them to take responsibility. Taking the initiative is crucial to turning plans into action. However, despite all efforts, luck still plays a role. It's important to acknowledge this, as it keeps us realistic and prepared. But of course, all said and done, you still need an element of luck for sure.

The Transformative Power of Stepping Out

Stepping out of your comfort zone and taking calculated risks is paramount in the journey towards transformative success. However, this requires meticulous planning and strategic foresight. Without a concrete plan, your efforts are likely to falter.

Careful Planning and Problem Identification

The foundation of any successful endeavor lies in identifying a clear business problem to solve. This serves as the prerequisite for moving forward. Having a well-defined issue you are addressing and a realistic understanding of the landscape is essential.

Equally important is pinpointing an enterprise customer or a known client with this specific problem. Engaging with someone you know who faces a tangible issue ensures you are working on a realistic and significant challenge. This approach mitigates the risks associated with working on hypothetical problems or with unknown clients.

Developing and Executing a Plan

Once the problem and potential customer are identified, developing a comprehensive plan is next. This includes:

1. **Solution Development and Implementation**: Outline how you will develop, execute, and support the solution.
2. **Business Model**: Define the business model that will sustain your solution delivery.

3. **Team Formation**: Identify key individuals to form a capable and cohesive team.

Having a clear vision of how these elements will unfold as you progress. Detailed planning minimizes the risks and provides a roadmap for success.

Continuous Assessment and Mentorship

Assessing your progress and being ready to make course corrections is crucial. Set milestones to review whether your plan is effective and identify necessary adjustments. This proactive approach ensures you stay on the right path and adapt to changes or challenges.

Additionally, having a mentor or an external advisor can be invaluable. Someone not directly involved in the operations can provide objective insights, highlight potential issues, and validate your strategies. Their external perspective can be the key to identifying what's working and what needs improvement.

Creating Value Through Insight and Planning

By integrating these elements—calculated risk-taking, careful planning, realistic problem identification, and continuous assessment—the likelihood of success is greatly enhanced. Once successful, the value you create can open up numerous opportunities in the market. With insight, observation, and meticulous planning, operational success becomes tangible.

Warning Against Paralysis by Analysis

While meticulous planning is crucial for success, it's equally important to avoid the trap of paralysis by analysis. Overanalyzing each planning stage or outcome can result in stagnation and hinder progress.

Pragmatism and Realism in Planning

Being pragmatic and realistic about what is achievable in your plan and the expected outcomes is essential. Experience plays a significant role in recognizing when to stop analyzing and start acting. Wisdom helps in managing situations effectively, especially when dealing with team dynamics.

Managing Team Dynamics

As an entrepreneur, you have the mental preparation to adapt and respond to challenges. However, your team members may have different levels of preparedness. They may not have taken the entrepreneurial leap with the same mindset and may feel uncertain about taking risks if things don't work out as planned.

Effective people management is vital to ensuring team cohesion and productivity. Keeping the team motivated and happy enhances their contribution to the project. A content and well-managed team will more likely generate innovative and effective solutions.

Balancing Analysis with Action

Rather than getting bogged down in excessive analysis or judgment, it's important to remain mentally prepared for course corrections. Always have contingency plans ready. If one plan doesn't work, know your next steps. This proactive approach ensures you are always a few steps ahead and ready to handle any eventualities.

Wisdom in Decision Making

A certain amount of wisdom is necessary to make informed decisions at every planning stage. Balancing careful analysis with practical action will help overcome obstacles and keep the project moving forward.

By integrating these principles—avoiding over-analysis, maintaining pragmatism, managing team dynamics, and exercising wisdom in decision-making—you can more effectively navigate the complexities of entrepreneurship.

Overcoming Fear in the Entrepreneurial Journey

For aspiring entrepreneurs, particularly those with industry experience, overcoming fear is crucial in exploring the entrepreneurial journey. Leveraging your existing knowledge and expertise can mitigate many of these fears.

Leveraging Industry Experience

If you've been deeply involved in your previous work, you likely understand the importance of planning and the extent to which it is necessary. Leaders are expected to take charge of their business strategies in today's business environment. Organizations provide the resources, but the responsibility of planning and execution falls on the individual.

Creating and Validating Your Plan

Your portfolio might be predetermined in an employment context. However, an entrepreneur must create a portfolio based on market knowledge and customer insights. This is where your experience becomes invaluable. Validate your ideas and plans with potential customers to ensure they meet market needs. Reviewing and setting milestones is crucial for staying on track and overcoming fears.

Embracing Risk and Uncertainty

No job, even in large organizations, is free of unknown factors. 80% of the variables are known, while 20% remain uncertain. This 20% of unknowns can drive significant changes and require adaptability. If 80% of your entrepreneurial plan is well-covered and validated, the remaining 20% can be managed with course corrections. Accepting and planning for this level of risk is essential.

Risk Management Strategies

To mitigate risks, consider the following strategies:

1. **Course Correction**: Be prepared to make adjustments as needed. A flexible plan allows for timely corrections if mistakes occur.
2. **Economic Activities**: If your venture is capital-intensive or time-consuming, incorporate economic activities that provide steady revenue. This ensures you remain operational and continue interacting with customers.
3. **Plan B**: Always have a backup plan. Even if it's not your core strategy, having a secondary plan can provide financial stability and support.

Capitalizing on Opportunities

Opportunities for value creation abound in a growing economy. The key is to be observant and innovative in delivering cost-effective solutions. Focus on optimizing your offerings without compromising on value.

Combining industry experience with strategic planning, embracing manageable risks, and remaining adaptable allows you to overcome fear and embark on a successful entrepreneurial journey. The market is ripe with opportunities for those prepared to observe, plan, and execute effectively.

This is your call for action: As we conclude this chapter, take a moment to reflect on what your entrepreneurial fears are. Write them down, confront them, and start mapping out your strategy to overcome them. Remember, the journey of a thousand miles begins with a single step. Let this be your first step.

Just like standing on the edge of that cliff, you have a choice. You can step back and wonder "what if," or you can spread your wings and dive into the exhilarating journey of entrepreneurship. As we move to the next chapter, "Crafting Your Entrepreneurial Vision," remember that overcoming fear is just the beginning. Now, it's time to envision where those wings can take you.

Chapter 2

CRAFTING YOUR ENTREPRENEURIAL VISION

"The vision must be followed by the venture. It is not enough to stare up the steps; we must step up the stairs."

— Vance Havner

Envision a world where every step you take is on a path illuminated by your deepest passions and highest aspirations. This isn't a fantasy—it's the power of a well-crafted entrepreneurial vision. Let's embark on the journey of transforming dreams into actionable goals that pave the way to success.

A clear, compelling vision is the north star for any successful entrepreneur. It guides decisions, fuels motivation, and shapes the future of a business. This chapter explores the importance of defining your vision and aligning it with your entrepreneurial endeavors for lasting impact and fulfillment.

Now that you've crystallized your vision, the next step is execution. How do you bring your idea to life? The question you should ask yourself is: What's the plan to realize this vision? Formulate a strategy, explore solutions, and dig deeper into the "why" behind your idea. Why is this concept essential? What difference will it make in the business landscape? Nietzsche once said, "He who has a why to live for can bear almost any how." This principle holds true in business, too. Success isn't just about setting a goal; it's about fostering a goal-driven mindset, complete with a plan and roadmap that guide you toward your destination.

Entrepreneurship often comes with the perception of risk. Critics may say, "That person is gambling with their future." But what's wrong with taking calculated risks when you understand the rules of the game? In a way, working for an established company is no different. How do you know that the organization you work for today will thrive tomorrow? Both scenarios involve risk, but the difference lies in ownership. With entrepreneurship, you're in control, creating your own roadmap to success.

René Descartes' famous quote, "I think, therefore I am," rings true in business as well. How you perceive your entrepreneurial journey is critical. If you view it as a gamble, it will feel uncertain and risky. But if you approach it with purpose and structure, you can build something enduring. You can't construct a lasting empire on shaky ground—your foundation needs to be solid and stormproof.

As Katie Thurmes wisely said, "You can't do a good job if your job is all you do." Entrepreneurship isn't merely about creating an income stream; it's about building a legacy. It transcends the day-to-day grind, becoming a higher purpose. You're not just working to generate profit—you're shaping your future, crafting your identity, and cementing your place as the architect of your own success. Your name on the doormat signifies more than ownership; it represents the legacy you're building.

A Case Study of Zoom: Embracing Small-Scale Entrepreneurship

Not every entrepreneur starts with grandiose ambitions. Many begin with a vision tailored to their local contexts and gradually build their empires. A prime example of this is **Zoom**, founded by Eric Yuan in 2011. Yuan's journey to success was not without significant struggles and setbacks.

Struggle and Early Days

Eric Yuan initially faced significant obstacles. Before moving to the U.S., his visa was rejected nine times. Determined to pursue his dreams, Yuan finally moved to California, where he worked at WebEx, a video conferencing company that was later acquired by Cisco Systems. Despite playing a pivotal role at WebEx, Cisco rejected Yuan's idea for a smartphone-friendly video conferencing system. Frustrated but undeterred, Yuan left Cisco in 2011 to start his own company—a story of failure before success.

Success and Growth

Yuan's vision for Zoom, initially named Saasbee, Inc., was to create a user-friendly, high-quality video conferencing tool. Launched in 2013, Zoom quickly differentiated itself with features that worked well on mobile devices and low bandwidth. Zoom's freemium model played a significant role in its widespread adoption, attracting millions of users within months and leading to significant venture capital funding.

By 2017, Zoom had reached a $1 billion valuation, and its growth continued at a rapid pace. The company's success skyrocketed during the COVID-19 pandemic when the demand for video conferencing solutions surged. Daily users soared to over 200 million, cementing Zoom's place as a leader in the industry.

Zoom's Key Success Factors

Zoom's rapid rise to success can be attributed to several key factors:

1. **User-Focused Design**: From the outset, Zoom was designed with the user experience in mind. The platform is easy to use, with intuitive interfaces that require minimal technical expertise. This focus on simplicity made it accessible to a wide range of users, from large enterprises to educational institutions and individual users.
2. **Scalability and Reliability**: Zoom invested heavily in building a robust and scalable infrastructure. This ensured that the platform could handle a large number of concurrent users without compromising on performance or reliability. During the COVID-19 pandemic, when demand for video conferencing surged, Zoom's infrastructure was able to support the massive influx of users seamlessly.
3. **Freemium Model**: Zoom's freemium pricing model played a significant role in its widespread adoption. By offering a free tier with essential features, Zoom allowed users to experience the platform's benefits before committing to a paid plan. This strategy not only attracted individual users but also encouraged businesses to adopt Zoom for their communication needs.

4. **Continuous Innovation**: Zoom continuously evolves its platform by adding new features and improving existing ones. By staying ahead of market trends and listening to user feedback, Zoom has maintained its competitive edge and remained relevant in a fast-paced industry.
5. **Community and Social Responsibility**: During the pandemic, Zoom provided free services to schools and educational institutions, supporting remote learning worldwide. This initiative not only showcased Zoom's commitment to social responsibility but also built strong brand loyalty and trust.

Lessons from Zoom's Journey

Zoom's story is a powerful example of how determination, innovation, and a user-centric approach can drive success. Yuan's journey from multiple visa rejections to founding a billion-dollar company exemplifies the resilience and perseverance needed to overcome obstacles.

The key takeaways from Zoom's success include:

1. **Start Small, Think Big**: Yuan identified a specific need in the market and addressed it with a well-designed solution. His ability to 'think big while starting small' allowed Zoom to grow organically and rapidly.
2. **Embrace Failure**: Yuan's idea was rejected at Cisco, but he used this setback as motivation to pursue his vision independently. Embracing failure as a learning opportunity can lead to greater achievements.
3. **Focus on the User**: Zoom's success is primarily due to its user-friendly design and continuous improvement based on user feedback. Keeping the user at the center of product development ensures relevance and satisfaction.
4. **Scalability is Key**: Building a scalable and reliable infrastructure allowed Zoom to handle explosive growth during

the pandemic, demonstrating the importance of preparing for future demands.
5. **Give Back to the Community**: Zoom's social responsibility initiatives during the pandemic enhanced its reputation and built trust. Businesses that contribute to their communities often gain loyal supporters.

Examples like Zoom show us that entrepreneurial success is not a one-size-fits-all journey. Whether you're starting with a grand vision or a modest goal, the ability to adapt, innovate, and persevere is crucial. Zoom's story demonstrates that success can be achieved through user-focused design, scalable infrastructure, strategic pricing, continuous innovation, and social responsibility. These principles offer a valuable blueprint for aspiring entrepreneurs everywhere, showing that with the right mindset and approach, remarkable success is attainable.

Exercises for Personal and Business Purposes

To embark on your personal and entrepreneurial journeys with practical insights and achievable goals, we include the following exercises. These exercises are aimed at helping you identify your personal and business purposes, encouraging reflection on individual motivations, and aligning them with meaningful business goals. This introspective approach fosters clarity and purpose in entrepreneurial pursuits.

Exercise 1: Personal Reflection

1. **Identify Your Passion**:
    - What activities or topics excite you the most?
    - What issues do you feel most passionate about solving?
    - How do these interests align with potential business opportunities?

2. **Assess Your Strengths and Weaknesses**:
   - What are your core strengths and skills?
   - What areas do you need to improve or seek support in?
   - How can you leverage your strengths to create a successful business?

3. **Define Your Vision and Mission**:
   - What is your long-term vision for your personal and professional life?
   - What mission statement can you create that encapsulates your purpose and goals?

Exercise 2: Business Purpose

1. **Market Research and Validation**:
   - Identify a specific problem or need in the market that resonates with your passions and strengths.
   - Conduct market research to validate the demand for your proposed solution.
   - Who are your potential customers, and what are their pain points?

2. **Create a Value Proposition**:
   - What unique value can your business offer to address the identified problem?
   - How will your product or service stand out from existing solutions?

3. **Set Meaningful Goals**:
   - Define short-term and long-term goals for your business.
   - How do these goals align with your personal vision and mission?
   - What milestones will help you measure progress and success?

4. **Develop a Business Plan:**
    - Outline the key components of your business plan, including your value proposition, target market, competitive analysis, marketing strategy, and financial projections.
    - How does each element of your business plan support your overall purpose?

By engaging in these exercises, you can gain a deeper understanding of both your personal and business purposes. This introspective approach will help you build a business that not only achieves financial success but also brings fulfillment and meaning to your entrepreneurial journey.

Let's explore the visions that have led other giant entrepreneurs to their success.

Elon Musk: A visionary in the tech world, Elon Musk has made an indelible mark with his forward-thinking ventures. One of his primary visions is the sustainability of the global economy, which can be seen in the development of Tesla. Tesla's focus on electric vehicles isn't just aimed at transforming the American market—it's about revolutionizing transportation on a global scale. By employing a direct-sales approach, Tesla cuts out the middleman, enabling them to reach customers worldwide with less overhead. The result is a broader, more accessible customer base. Similarly, Musk's Starlink initiative, which provides global satellite internet services, doesn't rely on partnerships to expand its market reach. This independence has shown its real-world impact, as demonstrated during the Russo-Ukraine war, where Starlink played a crucial role in maintaining communication amid the conflict.

Another key part of Musk's vision is tackling large-scale, complex problems. Musk has an eye for solving issues that others overlook. For instance, The Boring Company was created to address the urban gridlock that plagues cities worldwide. By focusing on building extensive underground tunnel networks, Musk aims to reduce traffic congestion significantly. His approach isn't just about finding solutions but doing so in a cost-effective and efficient way. Similarly, Neuralink is addressing the profound challenge of helping people with disabilities communicate and interact—a problem that has existed for centuries, but Musk saw an innovative way to solve it.

Musk also embraces vertical integration, a strategy where companies maintain control over their supply chains. In the case of SpaceX and Tesla, nearly every component is built in-house. This ensures higher quality control, greater adaptability, and the ability to maintain technological secrecy—an essential advantage for staying ahead of competitors. It also allows Musk's companies to innovate at a faster pace while keeping their proprietary technology secure.

One of Musk's most audacious visions is the concept of a multi-planetary civilization. The idea of humans living on other planets has long captured our imaginations, but Musk is actively working to make it a reality through SpaceX. The potential benefits of such a vision are immense, from tapping into untapped resources in space to advancing humanity's understanding of the universe. Colonizing other planets could also be a necessary step toward ensuring the long-term survival of humanity.

Carvana: On the other hand, we can look at Carvana, the second-hand car dealership giant in the U.S., as a cautionary tale of how important it is to safeguard a business against potential risks. Carvana enjoyed tremendous success for a period, fueled by its promise of delivering affordable cars anytime, anywhere. However, when the COVID-19 pandemic led to a surge in demand, coupled with stimulus checks flowing into the hands of consumers, Carvana was unable to keep up with its commitments. This caused a ripple effect of rushed orders, resulting in lawsuits that tarnished the company's brand image. The pressure to meet demand led them to purchase cars at higher prices from dealerships, further straining their financial situation. Over time, this resulted in a debt burden that compounded the company's problems, leading to employee turnover and operational struggles.

However, the Carvana story doesn't end there. Despite these challenges, the company has shown resilience, with its stock climbing from $10.60 USD on May 16th, 2023, to $120.41 USD on May 9th, 2024. This recovery underscores the importance of having a vision that adapts to adversity. Though Carvana's early promises caused operational strain, the company's ability to adjust and bounce back speaks to the resilience that entrepreneurs must cultivate in their journeys.

These examples illustrate the power of vision in entrepreneurship, whether it's Elon Musk's transformative ideas or Carvana's ability to recover from missteps. With a clear purpose and a keen sense of direction, you can build a business that not only achieves financial success but also leaves a lasting impact on the world.

Building a Vision-Driven Business: A Case Study

While impactful examples like Elon Musk and other major players are essential to understanding the heights of entrepreneurial success, it's also crucial to highlight more relatable examples from domestic markets. Not every entrepreneur starts with grandiose ambitions akin to Musk's ventures. Many begin with a vision tailored to their local contexts and gradually build their empires.

Take Zoho, for instance. Founded by Sridhar Vembu in 1996, Zoho started as a modest software development firm in India. Unlike the colossal beginnings of some tech giants, Zoho's journey is a testament to the power of slow and steady growth. Vembu and his team focused on creating valuable software solutions for businesses, carving out a niche in the competitive tech industry.

Zoho's commitment to bootstrapping and organic growth is particularly inspiring. Without relying on external funding, the company has grown to serve millions of users globally, offering a suite of over 45 integrated applications. Their approach highlights that with dedication, innovation, and a deep understanding of customer needs, it's possible to build a successful and sustainable business from the ground up.

Zoho's Win-Win Philosophy

Zoho's success can be attributed to its win-win philosophy, which benefits both the company and its stakeholders. Here are the key aspects of this approach:

1. **Customer-Centric Development**: Zoho prioritizes the needs and feedback of its customers. By listening to their users and continuously improving their products, Zoho ensures that their software remains relevant, useful, and effective. This customer-centric approach builds loyalty and trust, creating a mutually beneficial relationship.
2. **Employee Empowerment**: Zoho invests in its employees, fostering a culture of innovation and continuous learning. By providing opportunities for professional growth and development, Zoho ensures that its workforce is motivated and skilled. This, in turn, leads to higher productivity and creativity, benefiting both the employees and the company.
3. **Sustainable Growth**: Zoho's decision to remain bootstrapped and avoid external funding allows for sustainable growth. Without the pressure of meeting investors' short-term expectations, Zoho can focus on long-term goals and maintain its independence. This approach ensures that the company can make decisions that are in the best interest of its customers, employees, and the business itself.
4. **Community Engagement**: Zoho is committed to giving back to the community. The company's initiatives in rural education and employment provide opportunities for underprivileged

communities, fostering economic growth and development. This social responsibility not only enhances Zoho's brand image but also creates a positive impact on society.
5. **Affordable Solutions**: Zoho offers high-quality software at affordable prices, making it accessible to small and medium-sized businesses (SMBs). By providing cost-effective solutions, Zoho helps SMBs compete with larger enterprises, fostering a more equitable business environment.

By including examples like Zoho, we can illustrate that entrepreneurial success is not a one-size-fits-all journey. Whether you're starting with a grand vision or a modest goal, what's important is the ability to adapt, innovate, and persevere. Zoho's win-win philosophy demonstrates that success can be achieved through sustainable practices, customer focus, and social responsibility, offering a blueprint for aspiring entrepreneurs everywhere.

The Business Purpose: Creating Value

Any business should be to create value. While profitability naturally follows successful operations, the primary focus should be solving real-world problems. This approach not only ensures sustainability but also fosters innovation and continuous improvement. In dynamic economic environments, whether experiencing growth or downturns, opportunities abound for businesses that address pressing challenges.

Seizing Market Opportunities

During periods of economic expansion, businesses require more services and solutions. For instance, in the I.T. sector, there is increased demand for outsourcing and specialized services. Conversely, during economic contractions, cost-cutting measures and efficiency improvements become critical. Adapting to these market dynamics presents opportunities to optimize operations and enhance profitability.

Personal Purpose: Challenging Oneself

From a personal perspective, transitioning from secure leadership roles to entrepreneurship involves embracing challenges and self-discovery. Securing resources and approvals within established organizations necessitates strategic planning and persuasion. Similarly, in entrepreneurship, external funding hinges on presenting compelling business plans. The goal remains consistent: to prove oneself capable of creating substantial value, securing customer loyalty, and achieving sustainable growth.

Embracing Growth and Learning

Challenging oneself in an entrepreneurial context involves applying accumulated knowledge and skills to new ventures. It's about experimenting, learning from mistakes, and continuously evolving. Personal growth stems from overcoming challenges, leveraging strengths, and addressing weaknesses to foster professional development and business success.

Value Creation and Market Recognition

Ultimately, the measure of success lies in operational returns and the enduring value created for customers and stakeholders. Building a solid customer base, establishing a market presence, and generating a positive impact are pivotal in attracting potential investors or buyers. This underscores the significance of creating tangible value and solving real-world problems as the core purpose of entrepreneurship.

By aligning business endeavors with meaningful problem-solving and personal growth objectives, entrepreneurs can navigate challenges, capitalize on opportunities, and significantly contribute to their industries and communities.

However, the entrepreneurial path is far from simple if you lack a clear plan and the drive to pursue your goals. It's obvious: without a map, the chances of stumbling upon treasure are slim. Throughout history, every successful explorer has had a cartographer by their side, carefully charting the course because it's just as important to know how you got somewhere as it is to know what you did to get there. The same applies to building a start-up. Like the adventurers of old, you may not know every detail of how to reach your ultimate destination, but you can learn from the journeys of others, using their successes and failures to map out your own controlled path.

Consider it like watching those air crash investigation shows on National Geographic. By examining where pilots went wrong, we learn valuable lessons, ensuring that the same mistakes aren't repeated. Similarly, in entrepreneurship, there are constant markers that signal whether you're headed in the right direction. The key is to be aware of these signs and understand the path you're on.

If your company is struggling, you'll see red flags, such as a lack of product-market fit. This often happens when a product is launched with incomplete research, leading to inflated expectations that don't match public interest. When early adopters react poorly, negative publicity can severely damage your brand. Another sign of trouble is the depletion of funds. Financial mismanagement can cause businesses to panic-spend in an attempt to salvage things, only to dig a deeper hole, resulting in even greater losses.

Lack of traction is another common issue. Without a solid customer base, a company will stagnate and eventually fail. Infighting within leadership can also signal that the foundation of the company is crumbling. As W.B. Yeats famously wrote, "Things fall apart; the center cannot hold." Poor money management is a frequent downfall for start-ups, as seen on shows like Shark Tank. Entrepreneurs who receive large sums of investment money often go on spending sprees without careful planning, leading to financial ruin.

Conflicts between investors and key stakeholders are also warning signs. If the leadership starts cutting ties with their financial backers, it's a signal that deeper issues may be at play, such as internal disagreements or changes in management. For an entrepreneur, this is a red flag, as you are often the leader whose vision guides the company.

High turnover rates and negative workplace culture are additional markers that the company is veering off course. And then there's the issue of focus—companies that jump from one product or service to another without a coherent strategy come across as desperate and disorganized. This erodes trust, making it difficult for the business to establish itself in the market. Inconsistent branding and poor marketing can also be devastating. Even the best products can be forgotten if they're not marketed well, leading to missed opportunities in a crowded marketplace.

As in sailing, these are your guiding stars, your sextant through the entrepreneurial storm. A strong, loyal customer base is vital, and maintaining that base should be a top priority to ensure the survival and success of your business.

Identifying a Market Gap

In our journey towards entrepreneurship, we identified a significant gap in the identity management sector. The existing environment was fragmented, lacking integration across various subsystems crucial for large enterprises. Recognizing this opportunity, we saw the potential to streamline operations and enhance data analytics capabilities through comprehensive integration solutions.

Bootstrapping and Strategic Initiatives

With limited financial resources, we opted for bootstrapping, funding our venture independently without external investors. This decision necessitated strategic planning and diversification to sustain our operations. We ventured into system integration services, which not only provided essential revenue but also deepened our understanding of the ecosystem, enabling us to refine our solution.

Diversifying Revenue Streams

To mitigate risks and bolster financial stability, we engaged in trading activities alongside our core operations. While trading served as a supplementary income source, our primary focus remained on developing and implementing robust identity management solutions. This dual approach allowed us to navigate early challenges and establish a foothold in the market.

Expanding into New Domains

Driven by our vision to innovate and solve critical business problems, we expanded into the transportation sector, particularly focusing on communication, signaling, and anti-collision systems for railways. This diversification not only broadened our service portfolio but also positioned us uniquely in an industry typically dominated by larger players.

Achieving Milestones and Recognition

Through persistence and strategic growth, we achieved significant milestones. Today, our company boasts a global presence with offices in India, the U.S., Europe, and Singapore. We support a diverse clientele worldwide, earning recognition from industry analysts such as Gartner for our pioneering solutions in identity management and transportation sectors.

Building a Resilient Organization

Central to our success has been our ability to build a resilient and cohesive team. Over the years, we have attracted top talent from the industry who share our passion for solving complex challenges. Our commitment to fostering a supportive work environment has resulted in high employee retention and a cohesive organizational culture.

Overcoming Challenges and Growth

Despite initial financial constraints, we navigated challenges by leveraging operational successes to secure additional funding and credit facilities. We succeeded in persuading talented professionals to join our ranks, drawn by the opportunity to contribute meaningfully to our vision-driven initiatives. Today, as we celebrate our tenth year, many of our original team members continue to play pivotal roles, underscoring our enduring commitment to growth and innovation.

Our journey exemplifies the transformative power of identifying market gaps, pursuing innovation, and building sustainable businesses driven by a clear vision. By focusing on creating value, diversifying revenue streams, and nurturing talent, we have not only survived but thrived in competitive markets. Looking ahead, we remain dedicated to expanding our footprint, delivering impactful solutions, and shaping the future of the industries we serve.

The idea of building your own personal business vision is, in a way, like confronting your innermost version of you. In the sense that you have to negotiate with what exactly you want your legacy to be in the business. The first step in setting the vision for your start-up is to identify your core values, which are the fundamental beliefs and guiding principles that define your behavior and actions. What idea are you going to carry into the market, what are you standing for, is your goal profit or solving problems? The reason to introspect your core values is that, for the most part, since the company is going to be an extension of you, it will be an extension of your legacy that will live on, so an intense introspection of your motives is something you should give into.

The subsequent step in formulating your vision is to define your goals. Where do you place the marker that signifies the end of your journey? Whether you envision your business as a marathon or a sprint, it's essential to set realistic goals. This ensures that you don't exhaust your resources prematurely, instilling confidence and security in your business journey.

Visualize the long term and make sure your goal is reasonable. Visualizing is good, but many people build castles in the clouds while visualizing. This is where visualizing goes too far, and this usually tends to cause a lot of heartbreak when it doesn't pan out. When visualizing, it's important to be specific and detailed. Imagine your business in operation, your team, your customers, and the impact you're making. This will help you to create a more realistic and achievable vision for your business.

Write down your vision statement. This is important since, a lot of the time, your vision statement begins to change based on the situation, which can lead to a more realizable plan. A vision statement is a concise and inspiring declaration that communicates the direction and aspirations of your business. For example, 'To be the leading provider of innovative solutions in our industry' or 'To create a world where everyone has access to clean energy.' This is why you must constantly review your vision statement. Another plus to this step is the idea that as you progress, you can check things out of the list; this will give you some motivation in your journey to success.

Defining Roles and Measuring Success in Organizational Building

Importance of Clarity in Roles and Responsibilities

When building an organization, it is crucial to establish clear roles and responsibilities for all team members. Without this clarity, managing the organization becomes exceedingly difficult. One book that offers valuable insights into this aspect is "Measure What Matters." This book emphasizes the importance of focusing on what truly matters at each stage of the organization's growth. It highlights how successful companies have used specific techniques to achieve their goals.

The key takeaway from the book is the need to identify and measure what is important at any given stage of the organization's development. Rather than getting bogged down by a plethora of metrics, it's essential to pinpoint the few critical measures that will drive success at that moment.

Goal Setting Aligned with Roles

Each year, the organization should set clear, actionable objectives. These goals should be specific to the roles and responsibilities of the team members. For instance:

- **Development Team**: The objective might be to ensure that new functionalities are developed, tested, and deployed efficiently, addressing any vulnerabilities that arise.
- **Sales Team**: The goal could be to establish and maintain relationships with a set of key large enterprises. This involves understanding their changing needs and feeding this information back to the development team. This approach ensures that when the solution is ready for deployment, it meets the market's requirements and can be piloted effectively.

Alignment with a Larger Vision

It's imperative that the goals and roles of key resources align with the organization's larger vision. This alignment ensures that every effort contributes towards the overarching objectives of the organization. By clearly defining what needs to be achieved and who is responsible for each task, the organization can move forward cohesively and effectively.

Building a successful organization requires more than just a vision; it requires meticulous planning and a clear delineation of roles and responsibilities. By focusing on what matters most at each stage and aligning individual goals with the organization's broader vision, leaders can ensure that their teams work efficiently and purposefully toward shared success.

SMART goals criteria help set clear, attainable goals in an organized manner, making it easier to stay on track and achieve success. SMART is an acronym for Specific, Measurable, Achievable, Relevant, and Time-bound goals.

- → **Specific:** Define a clear, focused goal with a vision that outlines exactly what outcome you want to achieve.
- → **Measurable:** The goal should be quantifiable, allowing you to track progress. Avoid vague metrics that change frequently; this ensures clarity on where you are and what steps to take next.
- → **Achievable:** Your goal must be realistic and attainable. Setting practical targets keeps you grounded and prevents frustration when fantasy-driven goals prove unattainable.
- → **Relevant:** Goals should align with your broader vision. Staying true to your objectives ensures your efforts remain purposeful, preventing you from veering off course.
- → **Time-bound:** Set a clear timeline for achieving your goal. Time is valuable, and having deadlines keeps you accountable and focused on reaching your target efficiently.

Goal Setting and Client Relationship Building in System Integration

Initial Focus on Specific Clients

When we embarked on our system integration journey, the primary goal for our system integration head was clearly defined: focus on two named clients. His responsibility was to ensure the successful delivery of all system integration tasks for these clients. The critical success factor was establishing a dependable service relationship where the client could confidently rely on us to complete any task assigned within the scope.

Building Dependability

The aim was to build a reputation as a reliable service provider in the system integration domain. These large enterprise accounts typically have annual budgets for various tasks. By focusing on a couple of key clients, we aimed to create a foundation of trust and dependability. This strategy meant we didn't need to search for new clients constantly; instead, we concentrated on delivering exceptional service to our chosen clients.

Expanding Scope and Revenue

In the second year, after establishing our dependability, the goal shifted to increasing revenue by expanding the scope of our services. This expansion allowed us to enhance our portfolio, capabilities, and domain expertise. The focus was on growing within our existing client base while showcasing our increased competencies.

Adding New Clients

By the third year, the objective evolved to include onboarding more large enterprise customers. The goal was not to add numerous clients but to selectively choose two or three qualitative customers with significant spending potential. The idea was to maintain a steady revenue stream from existing clients while focusing on incremental revenue from new clients. This selective approach ensured that we could add value and address specific issues within each new customer space, further solidifying our reputation.

Clear Goals for Each Phase

In the first year, the focus was solely on client coordination and task completion, with no pressure on revenue generation. The aim was to establish a strong presence and build trust with the clients. As we progressed, revenue responsibilities increased, but with a solid foundation of satisfied clients, achieving these goals became manageable.

Aligning Goals with Organizational Growth

It's crucial to align individual goals with the organization's broader objectives, especially in terms of growth. Setting unrealistic or irrelevant goals in the preliminary stages can be detrimental. Therefore, having clear, achievable goals that evolve with the organization's growth is essential for sustainable success.

By focusing initially on building dependable relationships with a few key clients and gradually expanding our scope and client base, we were able to create a robust and sustainable system integration business. Clear goal setting and aligning these goals with the organization's growth trajectory ensured that each phase of our journey was manageable and successful.

My journey into entrepreneurship is one that many young, budding entrepreneurs will find relatable. I initially embarked on this path out of sheer boredom with the corporate world. The routine nature of my job, with little to no added value or challenge, made me realize I was capable of so much more. The constraints of being an employee—the ever-shifting responsibilities that leave you with little time to think—forced me to confront a crucial decision. Do I continue with this mundane work, or do I pursue something that aligns with my potential?

The corporate world offers many opportunities for others who are suited to it, but I knew I wanted more. I didn't want to waste time, especially when I had the confidence that I could build something of my own. This realization led me to explore what was missing in my life and how I could turn that gap into an opportunity.

For me, the key was planning and budgeting. I needed to know my mission and understand the costs associated with achieving it. The initial phase of entrepreneurship didn't come with a clear timeline, so I had to find ways to keep progressing while waiting for the right moment. In my case, this meant involving myself in other ventures, such as trading, and maintaining momentum until the bigger picture started to take shape.

Challenging myself to find a path to success became my purpose. I wanted to build something that, in the end, would make the world take notice. The current boom in the start-up world provides wind in the sails for anyone embarking on this journey, but it only works if you have a solid plan and a strong compass to guide you. That's when I thought, why not experiment with this opportunity?

When you're part of an organization, there's a sense of security in the support system of colleagues. But it's crucial to recognize that there are communities and individuals outside the corporate environment who can offer the same guidance and support. This realization opened up new avenues for growth in my entrepreneurial ambitions. The lesson here is that you're never truly alone. Others have walked this path before you, and their experiences can be invaluable in shaping your own journey.

That's exactly what I did. I researched competitors and thought about how to differentiate my offering. The only way to truly stand out is to create your own unique solution. This gives you the key to solving problems that are specific to your situation, allowing you to stand as your own entity rather than a rebranded copy of someone else's idea.

We met our goals and targets well before the company reached its intended capacity. Of course, scaling a company requires finances, so we supplemented our resources by leveraging partnerships, trading, and other activities to keep the cash flow steady. In doing so, we were able to grow sustainably.

The process also provided opportunities to network with other players in the market, making the journey all the more enriching. This approach isn't groundbreaking, but it's effective. It involves continuously thinking, planning, and refining until you're fully immersed in the market you're entering.

In short, my journey wasn't just about breaking free from a dull job; it was about methodically planning, adapting, and positioning myself for long-term success, all while learning from others and staying true to my vision.

Vision-Driven Organizational Building

The Importance of a Clear and Compelling Business Need

A clear and compelling business need is the cornerstone of any successful vision. This need drives the creation of value and the solving of significant business problems, especially those pertinent to large enterprises. Identifying and addressing these needs is crucial for establishing a strong foundation for your organization.

Self-Challenge and Skill Assessment

As a leader, it's essential to continuously challenge yourself and assess the skills you bring to the table. Understanding your own shortcomings is equally important. If you identify gaps in your skill set, it's vital to find resources or team members who can complement these areas. This approach ensures that you have a well-rounded team capable of meeting diverse challenges.

Strategic Team Selection and Goal Alignment

Choosing the right team and assigning appropriate goals at the right time is fundamental. Each team member should have goals that align with the larger organizational objectives for the year. This alignment ensures that everyone is working towards a common vision in a step-by-step process, which is especially crucial during the building phase of an organization.

Resource Management and Financial Discipline

Building an organization often involves resource constraints, particularly in terms of financial resources. Effective fiscal management and discipline are paramount. This includes generating funds, managing cash flow, and making strategic decisions about reinvesting earnings. A disciplined approach to fiscal management helps maintain the organization's stability and supports its growth.

Step-by-Step Organizational Building

Building an enterprise is a gradual process. It requires careful planning and execution, especially when resources are limited. By taking a step-by-step approach, you can ensure that each phase of development is robust and sustainable. This methodical process helps in creating a solid organizational foundation, which can be scaled up as the enterprise grows.

Vision-Based Organizational Success

Ultimately, the success of a vision-driven organization lies in its ability to clearly define and pursue its goals, effectively manage its resources, and continually adapt to new challenges. By maintaining a clear vision and aligning team efforts toward common objectives, an organization can achieve sustainable success and growth.

This approach to organizational building emphasizes the importance of clear vision, strategic planning, and disciplined execution, ensuring that the enterprise is well-positioned to meet its goals and thrive in the competitive business landscape.

This is your call for action: Take some time today to reflect on what you want your entrepreneurial legacy to be. Start drafting your vision statement and consider how it aligns with your personal values. Remember, a clear vision is the first step towards a purposeful and impactful entrepreneurial journey.

With your vision now taking shape and illuminated by your passions and aspirations, the path ahead is clearer. But a vision without action remains a dream. As we transition to the next chapter, "Cultivating Discipline and Resilience," prepare to learn how to steadfastly walk your path, turning your visionary dreams into reality.

Chapter 3

CULTIVATING DISCIPLINE AND RESILIENCE

"Resilience is knowing that you are the only one that has the power and the responsibility to pick yourself up."

— **Mary Holloway**

Imagine the entrepreneurial journey as a marathon, not a sprint. The path is long and filled with ups and downs, requiring endurance, patience, and, most importantly, discipline and resilience. These qualities form your mental and emotional training regimen, preparing you not only to start the race but also to endure its challenges and cross the finish line with triumph. This chapter is about building that stamina—ensuring you have what it takes to weather any storm that comes your way.

The success of any entrepreneurial venture hinges on the ability to cultivate discipline and resilience. These traits aren't innate but are developed through consistent practice and the right mindset. Just like a runner training for a marathon, your entrepreneurial journey requires you to practice discipline daily and build resilience through every setback and challenge you encounter.

Entrepreneurial success is often a result of playing the long game. It's like chess—a game where each piece represents a decision, and each move is crucial. You need to think ahead, anticipate challenges and opportunities, and be willing to make sacrifices for long-term gains. Much like in a chess match, you may have to give up a piece to protect your endgame. The lesson here is not just in being strategic but in understanding the balance between short-term sacrifices and long-term success.

In entrepreneurship, as in chess, you cannot afford to be oblivious to the moves of your competitors or the challenges ahead. Discipline helps you focus on what matters most, allowing you to cut away anything that doesn't directly contribute to your goals. Like the seemingly insignificant pawn in chess, which can become a game-changer if promoted, the smallest details in your business can be the key to your success. The ability to prioritize and recognize what is essential is critical. Ego or arrogance will only make you lose sight of the bigger picture.

Think of your business as training for a marathon. Repetition is key. The success you seek comes from doing the same things day in and day out, consistently refining and improving until you are well-conditioned for the challenges ahead. Whether it's sunny or stormy, you stick to your training routine. Over time, this routine transforms you into someone with the endurance and focus needed to stand out among competitors. However, this doesn't mean the work stops once you achieve some success. The marathon of entrepreneurship doesn't end with a single victory; it continues as long as you remain in the race.

This discipline can be seen in the analogy of BoJack Horseman's famous scene, where a character struggles to run, only to be told by a passing jogger that "it gets easier, but you have to do it every day." That's the essence of entrepreneurship—pushing yourself forward, even when it's difficult, knowing that the consistency of your effort will eventually make it easier. Rewards are not guaranteed every day, but that's no excuse to quit.

In a way, the entrepreneurial journey mirrors life itself. After World War I, absurdist thinkers like Albert Camus suggested that life is repetitive and often devoid of inherent meaning, yet within the monotony, small moments of meaning emerge. This concept, outlined in The Myth of Sisyphus, resonates deeply with the entrepreneur's journey. The repetitive grind, the constant pushing of the boulder uphill, can feel endless. But within that grind, you find your purpose, your moments of success, and ultimately, your legacy.

This surrender to the repetitive nature of building a business demands discipline. Humans naturally resist monotony, yet entrepreneurship requires you to commit to a routine that may seem monotonous at times. However, sticking to your game plan, the one you crafted when you first envisioned your business, creates a structure that brings your goals into reality. Like Sisyphus, you find meaning in the repetition, knowing that the discipline you practice today is what will ultimately allow you to achieve the success you desire.

In short, the marathon of entrepreneurship is one of discipline, resilience, and consistency. The grind is inevitable, but within it lies the key to your ultimate success.

Discipline is undeniably critical in the entrepreneurial journey, particularly when starting a new venture with numerous constraints. In the pilot stages, you're faced with limited resources—whether it's financial capital, human resources, or access to talent. Your ability to manage these resources with discipline directly impacts the success and sustainability of your startup.

Financial discipline is perhaps one of the most important aspects. It's not just a buzzword but a foundational practice that ensures the longevity of your venture. By carefully managing funds, planning expenses, and keeping payments on time, you reduce the need for external funding and foster relationships that enhance your creditworthiness. When vendors trust you because of your financial track record, they are more willing to extend credit, reducing the immediate burden on your cash flow. This type of discipline makes a significant difference, especially when your startup is operating on a tight budget.

Beyond funds, the discipline extends to planning every other aspect of your business, including real estate, office space, and personnel. Creating a comfortable and functional work environment is essential, especially if you're drawing talent from established companies where employees are accustomed to certain standards. However, it's about striking a balance—being resourceful and efficient without overindulging in unnecessary luxuries that can drain finances.

When it comes to building your team, discipline plays a vital role in hiring the right people. In a startup, there's no room for chance or mediocrity; you need to bring in competent individuals who can contribute meaningfully. It's not just about finding inexpensive labor but about selecting talent that aligns with the vision and can help you solve the problems your business is targeting. For larger projects or complex endeavors, skilled project managers and specialists are essential. Without them, one small mistake could be enough to derail your progress, as even a minor misstep in execution can sink the ship.

Discipline also involves fostering strong connections with your team. Once you have the right people in place, retaining them becomes a top priority. This is achieved through emotional connection, shared goals, and consistent communication. Entrepreneurs must appreciate their team's contributions and build an environment of trust. In a startup, many employees join because they believe in the vision or want to take a calculated risk, but they need constant reassurance that the company is moving in the right direction. Open communication, regular feedback, and celebrating small wins are essential to keeping morale high and ensuring that everyone is aligned with the larger vision.

Communication within a startup isn't just a necessity; it's the lifeblood that keeps the organization moving. With a small team, every step and decision matters, and keeping everyone informed helps build confidence and unity. Regular updates, transparent decision-making, and ensuring the team feels connected to the company's progress are crucial to maintaining momentum.

Additionally, being resourceful and tapping into external networks can greatly enhance your ability to solve problems and move forward. Whether it's inviting experts for guidance or seeking external resources, your connections and industry relationships can play a pivotal role in addressing challenges beyond your team's expertise.

Entrepreneurs must remain adaptable and resourceful, handling unexpected challenges calmly without overreacting. Building a reliable team, delegating responsibilities, and maintaining discipline at every level are necessary for scaling the business. As your company grows, the need for a strong, disciplined team becomes even more important, ensuring that every part of the organization is functioning effectively. This way, you'll be able to build a strong foundation and expand sustainably rather than letting the weight of the work overwhelm you.

Ultimately, discipline in financial management, hiring, communication, and overall business planning forms the backbone of a successful entrepreneurial venture.

The first thing you need is a mindset for business planning. One of the first steps is to understand your motivation. You must understand it to the point where it keeps you in line. You wouldn't take up an Odyssey or a quest, only to give it up when the sky gets cloudy. Thus, your motivation for the goal has to be concrete to a point where you can bear any adversities. The reason for this journey shouldn't be built on a goal that can be blown away with the wind.

Set a measurable goal, and you need to find a goal to have you in a positive feedback loop. This is essential since even the most resilient person might be stuck in a problem where a failure can temporarily disrupt the present system. This sound system is in the initial phase of start-up development. This is because you initially need to enter the motion of the system you have set up to maintain a consistent form of success. This can help you remain motivated in the long run.

Be proactive. Examine and study the system repeatedly to find the weak links in its structure. This will help you confront the system's issues before they can cause a more significant problem later on. There could also be opportunities to form a clientele. It would help if you went out of your way to gain the client's trust. It's very backward thinking to expect things to go your way.

Know when to take risks. This goes back to the chess metaphor at the start of the chapter. You need to know when to sacrifice what piece. It would help if you were careful what you consider redundant and stop working on since some aspects of the business may seem trivial at the start but become essential very quickly, and there is little you can do about it. Sound judgment is vital to most of your acquisition of the client's confidence in your product and service.

Being persistent during the initial phase of your business formation is vital since you cannot put the pursuit of the endeavor's success to the forefront of your efforts. This is mainly because of the sacrifices you have already undertaken since you cannot pursue a career elsewhere while you run to begin a start-up. Thus, being a sacrifice of the highest order, you must put all your effort into the task. Also, there is no safety net if you do a sloppy job and have to return to where you started. This is why you have to reassess your motivation; if you are not sure why you're doing this, you will find it hard to be persistent. If you know why you're doing this and are familiar with your tasks, then you must be persistent.

Embrace the challenges since they are your obstacles to success, so if you're hitting walls, you're making headway toward success. Have a look at your predicament in this lens. You chose this endeavor because you were tired of being a cog in a system. Rather than being a system of your own now, that is what you have. Rather than running away from the complications of this absurdity, chase it. The more you overcome these barriers, the more you can finally overcome these obstacles, and the more you will be experienced in the field, which will lead you to succeed in finding future challenges as trivial.

Regain a clear focus on the goals you're looking towards. This is necessary as every challenge will make you question how badly you need this. The issue is that the more you run away from the difficulties presented to you by your endeavor, the more you end up despising the goals you set to make it so far. The idea is to make peace with the difficulties by remembering the results of each goal, as they will remind you how rewarding they were.

Embark on networking; it's a powerful tool for progress, and the connections you build will prove invaluable in the long run. A robust relationship with vendors and software specialists could work in your favor when you require similar services. Moreover, fostering a sense of camaraderie with other companies in similar positions can instill a feeling of unity. The aim is to forge alliances that can yield significant benefits over time. Consider the potential of bringing more seasoned industry members into your circle, potentially leading to a mentor-mentee dynamic where they guide your development over time.

Continual learning is critical, for, like the seas, the business world is very unpredictable, so you have to study the situation. The idea is that you spare no detail to chance. Over time, this will become trivial, the idea of a constant overview, but in the initial phase of the company, it will be more discernable since you've just risen from the ground up. It is like starting a small fishing endeavor where, at the start, you get a small troller. Noe in this small troller, you can feel every turbulent jutting of the sea. Over time, with more capital and good fortune at sea, you get a bigger boat, and you will notice less turbulence. Over time, you will have a great boat that will keep you safe. However, this doesn't mean you stop learning after all that. After being vigilant for this many years, two things happen: once, you get into the habit of being watchful. The second is that you might be appealed by the sunk cost fallacy, where you would want to slack on the project after this much effort.

Prudent risk management is a cornerstone of success. You don't want to risk losing much on a trivial win. The key here is to carefully weigh the pros and cons of every action or decision. This will enable you to determine what is truly essential at the moment and guide your resource allocation in the right direction.

Cultivating Discipline and Resilience

Financial Management and Discipline

In the face of financial hardships, disciplined financial management becomes crucial. Efficiently managing financial and human resources ensures that they are used optimally to achieve the organization's goals. During the initial stages of building an organization, it is vital to carefully plan and allocate limited financial resources to prevent unnecessary expenditures. This disciplined approach is fundamental to sustaining operations and supporting the development of solutions that add value to the business.

Bootstrapping and Service Funding

Our journey exemplifies the importance of disciplined resource management. We bootstrapped our operations, starting with system integration services and trading activities. These were not just revenue-generating endeavors but strategic moves to fund the development of our core solutions. By providing system integration services, we gained valuable insights and resources needed for building robust solutions to business problems.

Differentiating Through Service Excellence

In highly competitive service sectors like system integration, differentiation is key. Our commitment to delivering dedicated, faster, and smoother services sets us apart. For large engagements, our program management capabilities ensured successful implementations across diverse geographies and timelines. This approach built trust and reliability with our clients, which is essential when you lack a prior track record.

Strategic Financial Management

Financial challenges were a significant hurdle, as we chose not to seek external investment initially. Instead, we focused on demonstrating operational viability. By successfully acquiring customers and delivering solutions, we aimed to prove to potential investors that our approach was both feasible and valuable. This required strict financial discipline, avoiding unnecessary expenditures, and prioritizing investments that directly supported our goals.

Perseverance in Building Trust

Building a new enterprise requires perseverance, especially when convincing potential customers who might be hesitant due to your lack of background. Demonstrating consistency and perseverance is key to gaining trust and opportunities. It's about proving your capability through small tasks and gradually building a reputation for reliability and excellence.

Balancing Consistency and Adaptability

Maintaining consistency and perseverance while managing financial and people resources is a dynamic challenge. It requires a balance of steadfastness in pursuing goals and adaptability in response to changing circumstances. This approach ensures that the organization can navigate the complexities of growth and development effectively.

Cultivating discipline and resilience is essential in building a successful organization. It involves meticulous financial management, strategic service differentiation, and unwavering perseverance. By aligning these elements with the organization's goals and demonstrating consistent effort, an enterprise can overcome initial challenges and establish a strong foundation for sustainable growth.

Discipline is essential in introducing habits that can help in the long run. This comes with the sense that if you keep at something, no matter how unappealing, you will form it into a habit in the long run. That is the point of discipline. The fact is that establishing the routine can cause a progressive ascension to a higher working capacity. The progression rises through a push toward the right direction since perfecting a person's capacity is like crafting a Japanese sword. You must work through the fold and hammer it until you find a sharp edge. After this, you have to use it occasionally and polish it. These measures sound like a nagging burden, but it is essential to have a reliable sword. The same applies to you as a critical factor in your company.

The concept of discipline also helps you stay focused on your goals. It's common to start making ambitious plans as you progress towards success. This is like sailing and seeing an island on the horizon. You might start fantasizing about what you'll do when you reach the island without considering the distance between you and the island. This is what we call 'building castles in the clouds'-creating unrealistic expectations. To prevent this, you need the discipline to keep you grounded and focused on the reality of your starting point.

Efficiency and productivity are other facets where discipline helps iron out your character in this endeavor. This is because you are bound by the duty to your creation. Pareto's principle is essential and can help in a situation like this. This principle is beneficial in the realm of productivity.

The 80/20 rule is mainly used to identify the most productive inputs and make them the priority of your endeavor. By focusing on the most productive tasks (20 percent), which could yield (80 percent) of the results, you can optimize the system's efficiency to its capacity. A significant misinterpretation is that many people think that the 80/20 ratio is a rule. This is far from the truth, and the point is that you need to judge the most output-yielding tasks. This means the ratios can change based on the needs and requirements of the principle, looking into the functions that yield the best outcome. However, a flaw in the understanding of the system is that people look into the high-output tasks, overlooking the rest of the functions entirely. This needs to be improved regarding the situation since neglected tasks can add up. After which it could burden the system. Efficiency means prioritizing the high-yielding tasks but accomplishing the tasks that seem mundane once the high-priority ones are done.

With a disciplined mindset, you become more agile and adaptable. For instance, if you're running a business and you're disciplined in your financial management, you'll be better prepared to handle unexpected expenses. Similarly, if you're disciplined in your time management, you'll be more flexible to accommodate changes in your schedule. This adaptability can be a significant advantage in the long run.

The Importance of Communication and Progress Tracking

Effective Communication with Co-Workers

Building an organization requires clear and consistent communication with co-workers. This communication keeps them motivated and engaged in their tasks. Regular updates on the company's progress help employees understand how their contributions are making a difference. By showing measurable improvements, you can boost team morale and reinforce their commitment to the organization.

Periodic Progress Updates

Periodic communication about progress is crucial. Sharing how the organization was performing a month ago compared to now provides a tangible measure of improvement. This can be highly motivating for employees as it shows that their efforts are leading to real advancements. Regular updates on key milestones, such as acquiring a new customer or securing a significant partnership, help employees see the value of their work.

Measuring and Sharing Achievements

Whenever possible, base communication on measurable facts. For instance, acquiring a new customer or securing a larger contract are clear indicators of progress. Partnering with a major OEM (Original Equipment Manufacturer) or a large company is a significant validation of your value proposition and can boost team confidence. Sharing these achievements helps employees feel more connected to the organization's success.

Motivation through Visibility

Providing visibility into the progress and the impact of employees' contributions is vital for motivation. Whether they are senior or junior resources, knowing that their work directly influences the company's success keeps them more involved and committed. This increased involvement leads to better performance and a more cohesive team effort.

Building a Success Story Together

For initial co-workers who took a chance on the organization, seeing measurable progress and being part of a success story is particularly important. Regularly communicating achievements and milestones helps them feel validated in their decision to join the company. This sense of belonging to a successful venture can drive them to contribute even more effectively.

In summary, effective communication and regular progress tracking are essential in building a motivated and engaged team. By sharing measurable achievements and providing visibility into the organization's growth, leaders can keep their employees motivated and invested in the company's success. This approach not only enhances individual contributions but also fosters a strong, cohesive team dedicated to achieving the organization's goals.

It must be said more to prioritize your health. To be productive, you have to have a good balance of exercise. This helps with cognitive procedures and also helps maintain the fitness you need to carry through your day-to-day. This also helps in de-stressing; the idea is to avoid carrying your job stress home. You must set a boundary between work time and my time since overstressing can weigh on you. They can overburden you to a point where you can get burnt out.

Setting realistic work limits is crucial. It's important to let go of the delusion that you can move a mountain in a single evening alone. Over time, you need to realize that you need rest. An excellent way to do this is to de-mark places with the designated task. For example, you could attend to work tasks at the office and delegate personal tasks at home. This could also allow you to have a life outside the office, which may sound trivial but is essential in the long run for your mental well-being. Tasks that can be delegated include administrative work, routine tasks, and tasks that don't require your specific expertise.

Empower your team by delegating minor decisions. This not only relieves you from the stress of making every decision but also fosters a more relaxed and collaborative work environment. Trusting your team with these decisions shows that you value their input and respect their abilities, leading to a more harmonious and productive workspace.

Recognizing the efforts of those around you is not just a nice gesture; it's a powerful tool for creating a positive work environment. It makes the workplace a welcoming space where you can enjoy your time. This contradicts the system of just surrendering to the call of duty. Since we all know that man is no island and thus desires the urge to communicate and reach out. Base communication and a pat on the back are sometimes reassuring enough to instill the idea that your efforts are being recognized. This feeling will make anyone feel nice and can significantly boost morale and productivity.

Maintaining and Motivating Your Team

Building Personal and Emotional Connections

Once you have assembled a team, it's crucial to maintain and motivate them. Developing personal and emotional connections with your team members helps keep them engaged. Regularly appreciating their efforts and reinforcing the sense that the team is moving in the right direction boosts their confidence and motivation. Many employees may have taken a risk by joining a startup, so it's important to validate their decision by showing them the progress and successes achieved.

Regular Communication and Sharing Success

Consistent communication is essential. Keeping team members informed about every step forward reassures them that their contributions are meaningful and that the organization is progressing. This is particularly important in a small startup environment where the impact of each individual's work is more visible. Sharing even small achievements can help maintain motivation and confidence.

Leveraging External Resources

Utilizing external resources can also be beneficial. Bringing in guest speakers or industry experts to solve specific issues or provide guidance shows employees that there is support available beyond the immediate team. This approach can help address challenges and provide fresh perspectives, reinforcing the sense that the organization is well-connected and capable of overcoming obstacles.

Staying Resourceful and Resilient

Being resourceful and maintaining a calm demeanor in the face of challenges is critical for a leader. By staying composed and open to unexpected situations, you can better navigate the uncertainties of building an organization. Responding to challenges with a positive attitude encourages the team to do the same and fosters a problem-solving culture.

Building a Collaborative Team

As the organization grows, it becomes increasingly important to delegate responsibilities and build a collaborative team. Sharing tasks and responsibilities ensures that no single person is overwhelmed and that the organization can scale effectively. A strong, cohesive team is essential for sustained growth and success.

Maintaining and motivating a team in a startup environment requires building personal and emotional connections, regular communication, leveraging external resources, staying resourceful and resilient, and fostering a collaborative team culture. By focusing on these aspects, leaders can ensure their team remains engaged, motivated, and confident in the organization's direction, ultimately contributing to its success.

Discipline is the foundation of resilience; the idea of doing a task in a greater sense of repetition is the primary motion of operation that resilience is known to be. Thus, if you are disciplined, you can easily be resilient. The definition of the two is intertwined like the ouroboros, where the start of defining one leads to the definition of the other. The idea is to form a mental headspace that will not be easily waived from the task. The idea of partaking in a task that is repetitive and precise is a good place to start. It helps you stay focused on your goals, maintain a positive mindset, and develop effective coping mechanisms.

Fostering a strong relationship with your work partners and the networks you have formed in the business arena. This can help create a good headspace and resilience, seeing that so much camaraderie supports you. At the same time, the networks in the same place as you can help make you realize that you are in this together. Also, the interactions between the members of your personal and professional circles can help you alter the perception of the magnitude of your challenges, giving you a more positive approach to overcoming your setbacks.

Self-awareness and empathy can help when the team is at an all-time low. Empathy may not come naturally to most team members, which is why it rests upon the leader to implement the concept of self-awareness. The leader had to pay attention and assess the chain of command to see if the team's strands were lagging because of workplace matters. The leader has to be able to break down barriers that would alienate the team members from the members in charge. Upon the reduced barriers, build a foundation of trust and transparency.

Cultivate a more open system when it comes to speaking one's mind on the matter. A sense of candor can help the team be open to each other since there cannot be a faulty cog in the greater engine. This has to work with everyone, knowing that they are in this together. And that there cannot be a sense of superiority.

Case Study: Freshworks

Struggle and Early Days

Freshworks, founded by Girish Mathrubootham and Shan Krishnasamy in 2010, emerged from Mathrubootham's frustration with existing customer support software. He experienced firsthand the inefficiencies and high costs associated with the solutions available at the time and saw an opportunity to create something better. Pooling their savings, Mathrubootham and Krishnasamy launched Freshworks with the vision of providing user-friendly, affordable customer support software.

However, the initial days were fraught with challenges. The founders faced significant hurdles in gaining traction and securing funding. The market was crowded with established players, making it difficult for a new entrant to stand out. Additionally, convincing potential investors to back their vision proved to be a formidable task. Their big break came when Freshworks was selected for Accel's startup accelerator program. This opportunity provided crucial funding, mentorship, and a network of contacts that helped the company navigate the startup landscape.

Failures and Comebacks

The journey of Freshworks was marked by multiple failures and setbacks that tested the resilience and determination of its founders:

1. **Initial Skepticism**: Gaining the trust of potential customers was a major challenge. Many were skeptical of a new entrant in a market dominated by established players. Convincing businesses to switch to Freshdesk required persistent efforts and a clear demonstration of value.
2. **Funding Struggles**: Securing initial funding was another significant hurdle. Many investors were wary of investing in a crowded market. Mathrubootham and Krishnasamy had to face numerous rejections before finally securing a place in Accel's startup accelerator program, which provided the much-needed financial boost.
3. **Technical Challenges**: Building a robust, scalable product with limited resources was a daunting task. The team faced numerous technical challenges and had to iterate rapidly to ensure their product met the high standards expected by users.
4. **Market Competition**: Competing with established giants in the customer support software market was a constant uphill battle.

Freshworks had to continuously innovate and differentiate itself to gain a foothold in the market.
5. **Operational Hurdles**: Scaling operations to meet the growing demand posed significant challenges. Ensuring consistent quality, managing a growing team, and maintaining efficient processes required constant vigilance and adaptation.

Despite these challenges, Freshworks' commitment to its vision never wavered. Girish Mathrubootham and Shan Krishnasamy undertook several strategic measures to overcome setbacks and push forward:

1. **Participating in Accel's Startup Accelerator**: This pivotal moment provided Freshworks with crucial funding, mentorship, and access to a network of industry experts. The support from Accel was instrumental in helping the company refine its product and business model.
2. **Focus on Customer Feedback**: Freshworks placed a strong emphasis on listening to customer feedback. By rapidly iterating on their product based on user input, they were able to address pain points and deliver a solution that truly met the needs of their target market.
3. **Strategic Product Development**: The launch of Freshdesk, their flagship product, was a game-changer. Its user-friendly interface and affordable pricing quickly gained traction among small and medium-sized businesses (SMBs). This success provided the momentum needed to expand their product line strategically.
4. **Building a Strong Team**: Freshworks invested in building a talented and dedicated team. Their collective efforts and expertise were critical in overcoming technical challenges and scaling operations.
5. **Persistence and Adaptability**: The founders' persistence and ability to adapt to changing circumstances were key to their success. They learned from each setback, adapted their strategies, and continued to push forward with determination.

6. **Discipline and Resilience**: Discipline in executing their strategies and resilience in the face of adversity was crucial for Freshworks. The founders maintained a disciplined approach to managing resources, developing products, and scaling operations. Their resilience helped them endure and recover from setbacks, ensuring that the company remained focused on its long-term goals.

Success and Growth

These efforts paid off. Freshworks' breakthrough came with the launch of Freshdesk, which rapidly gained popularity. Building on this success, Freshworks expanded its product line to include Freshservice, Freshsales, and other software solutions. Each product adhered to the same principles of usability, affordability, and functionality, tailored specifically for SMBs. This strategic focus on SMBs helped Freshworks carve out a significant niche in the SaaS market.

The company's growth trajectory was remarkable. By 2021, Freshworks had grown from a small startup to a significant player in the SaaS industry. Their growth was punctuated by their successful IPO on NASDAQ in 2021, a milestone that highlighted the company's evolution and solidified its position in the market.

Lessons from Freshworks' Journey

1. **Resilience in the Face of Failure**: Freshworks' story is a testament to the importance of resilience. Facing multiple failures and setbacks, the founders' determination to succeed drove them to overcome challenges and continue pushing forward.
2. **Customer-Centric Approach**: Listening to and acting on customer feedback was crucial to Freshworks' success. A customer-centric approach can help businesses create products that truly meet market needs and drive high satisfaction.

3. **Leveraging Opportunities**: Participating in Accel's startup accelerator program was a turning point for Freshworks. Leveraging such opportunities can provide valuable resources, mentorship, and industry connections.
4. **Focus on Core Values**: Freshworks' commitment to usability, affordability, and functionality was consistent across all its products. Staying true to core values can build a strong, authentic brand that resonates with customers.
5. **Adaptability and Innovation**: The ability to adapt and innovate was key to Freshworks' success. Continuously improving and expanding their product line helped them stay relevant and competitive.
6. **Discipline and Resilience**: Maintaining discipline in strategy execution and demonstrating resilience in the face of challenges were critical to Freshworks' success. These qualities ensured that the company stayed on course despite obstacles and setbacks.

Freshworks' journey from a struggling startup facing multiple failures to a major player in the SaaS industry is a powerful example of resilience, innovation, and strategic growth. Girish Mathrubootham and Shan Krishnasamy's determination to create user-friendly, affordable software for SMBs laid the foundation for their success. Their story provides valuable lessons for aspiring entrepreneurs, demonstrating that with the right approach, it is possible to overcome challenges, learn from failures, and achieve significant growth. Discipline and resilience played crucial roles in this journey, highlighting the importance of staying focused and committed to long-term goals despite short-term setbacks.

During my early days, challenges were aplenty, but none were more daunting than the financial hurdles we faced. Resources were scarce, and each step forward seemed to require a delicate balance of creativity, sacrifice, and careful maneuvering. While financial obstacles felt like the toughest to overcome, discipline and resilience were the cornerstones of our progress.

I learned quickly that discipline wasn't just about managing money; it was about following through on every commitment, walking the talk, and maintaining personal credibility. These values enabled us to build trust in the market. Today, our credibility stands strong, and it all traces back to the unwavering principle that a business, while focused on profit, must always honor its commitments.

If you're facing obstacles, remember that resilience and discipline are your most powerful allies. Commit to your goals and maintain your credibility, and success will follow.

This is your call for action: Identify one area in your entrepreneurial journey where you've felt challenged or overwhelmed. Commit to a small, daily discipline that will help you build resilience in this area. Remember, it's the small, consistent efforts that lead to big changes.

Just as a marathon runner prepares for the long race ahead, so must you equip yourself with discipline and resilience. With these qualities firmly in place, you're ready to move to the next phase of your journey: "Uncovering Your Unique Value Proposition." It's here that your disciplined approach and resilience will begin to differentiate you in the marketplace.

Chapter 4

UNDERSTANDING YOUR UNIQUE VALUE PROPOSITION

Your customers don't care about your solution; they care about their own problems.

– Dave McClure

In a sea of competitors, your unique value proposition (UVP) is the lighthouse that guides customers to your shores. It's what makes your business stand out, what makes customers choose you over others. This chapter is about discovering that beacon within your business, shining a light on what makes you unique.

Entrepreneur and Venture Capitalist

In a marketplace teeming with voices vying for attention, your unique value proposition (UVP) is the empowering beacon that cuts through the noise, drawing your ideal customers toward you. This chapter is dedicated to unveiling that distinct melody, the essence of what makes your entrepreneurial offering invaluable, discovering the beacon within your business, and shining a light on what makes you unique. By understanding and defining your UVP, you are not just navigating the competitive market but taking control of your business's narrative and positioning, empowering yourself to stand out.

In a sea full of fish (you will not just adhere to one species of fish, or in this case, only one particular solution provider), you look out for the most unique one, right? You don't just dive in and grab whatever you find closest to you. You float, maybe even swim, gathering all kinds of information the fishes give you. You take your time to choose the right partner, or well, in this case, the right solution provider. In an ocean of competitors, your unique value proposition (UVP) is the lighthouse that guides customers to your shores. It's what makes your business stand out, what makes customers choose you over others.

A well-defined UVP not only distinguishes you from competitors but also deeply resonates with your target audience, compelling them to choose you. Through meticulous strategic analysis and planning, we'll guide you in crafting a UVP that captures the heart of your business and speaks directly to your customers' needs and desires. This process is not about guesswork but about strategic decision-making and analysis, providing you with a solid foundation for your UVP and the confidence to stand out.

Every successful business rests on the foundation of a compelling, unique value proposition that clearly communicates why its product or service is better or different from the competition. For instance, Apple's UVP has an innovative design and user-friendly interface, which sets it apart from other technology companies. Similarly, Amazon's UVP of 'Earth's biggest selection and convenient shopping experience' has allowed it to dominate the e-commerce market. Identifying and articulating your UVP is not just about marketing; it's about deep self-awareness, understanding your strengths and weaknesses, and how you can leverage them to meet your customers' needs.

This chapter guides you through the process of uncovering and defining your UVP, ensuring it resonates with your target audience.

McClure, the founder of 500 Global, is a startup accelerator and seed fund. His quote reflects a common sentiment in the business and startup world, emphasizing the importance of focusing on the customer's needs and problems rather than just pushing a product or solution. It underscores the need for a customer-centric approach when defining your UVP. By putting your customers at the center of your UVP, you are not just showing them that their needs and problems are valued and understood but also fostering a stronger connection with them, making them feel appreciated and heard.

The 'journey to uncovering your UVP' starts with a deep dive into your strengths and passions. Understanding what you excel at and what drives you is not just crucial; it's a powerful tool for defining the value you bring to your customers. This journey involves self-reflection, market research, and strategic planning to identify your unique strengths and how they can be leveraged to meet your customers' needs.

A typical unique value proposition doesn't just identify a problem; it illuminates a path to resolution. Whether it's grappling with soaring expenses, inaccessible data formats, interoperability hurdles, or ensuring seamless day-to-day operations, these challenges invariably have a financial ripple effect. The essence of our value proposition lies in its direct alignment with addressing these economic concerns.

It is paramount to articulate effectively how our value proposition and solution translate into tangible financial benefits. It's about demonstrating how our offering either saves money or amplifies revenue streams, ultimately enhancing the bottom line. This clarity in communication is essential for potential clients to grasp the transformative impact our solution can have on their operations, recognize the value of our solution, and understand why they should adopt it.

Our value proposition has proven its mettle time and again in the crucible of real-world application. Take, for instance, our inaugural client engagement, where our solution engineered an impressive 32% slash in overall expenditure. This tangible outcome serves as a beacon of our efficacy, fostering enduring partnerships and trust with our clientele. Similarly, companies like Amazon, with their UVP of 'Earth's biggest selection and convenient shopping experience, 'have been able to dominate the e-commerce market.

Importance of a Unique Value Proposition

Experience in European Markets

The emphasis is on the importance of having a unique value proposition (UVP) for business success, particularly in crowded markets. They share their experience of initially struggling in the European market by using strategies that had worked in other regions like the US and the UK. The realization came that continental Europe required a different approach and positioning.

Challenges of Being a Generalist

For startups, being a generalist in a crowded market makes it challenging to stand out. This highlights the necessity of being seen as a specialist in a specific area to attract customers. Without a distinct UVP, it becomes difficult to gain recognition and business, as competing on general terms doesn't offer a significant advantage.

Building a Unique Value Proposition

Fidrox Technologies is focused on creating a UVP that was eventually recognized by Gartner as one of the few vendors in that niche. This recognition was achieved by identifying a unique solution that addressed a specific problem, providing significant benefits to customers.

Value Proposition over Cost

Competing solely on cost is unsustainable for long-term success. I keep stressing that a strong UVP, which solves a problem and offers substantial benefits, is a critical success factor. Differentiating the business through a unique solution rather than competing on price is essential for establishing a strong market presence.

Takeaways

1. **Identify a Unique Value Proposition:** As a startup, it is crucial to be a specialist in a specific area to stand out in a crowded market.
2. **Tailor Strategies to Specific Markets:** Different markets may require unique approaches and positioning strategies. What works in one region may not work in another.
3. **Build Recognition through Unique Solutions:** Creating a UVP that is recognized by industry leaders (e.g., Gartner) can validate the business's approach and attract more customers.

4. **Focus on Value Over Cost:** Competing on cost alone is challenging. Providing a unique solution that offers significant benefits is more sustainable and effective for long-term success.
5. **Constantly Evaluate and Adapt:** Continually reassess and refine the value proposition to ensure it remains relevant and effective in addressing customer needs and market demands.

Action Items

- Identify a UVP where the business is seen as a specialist in a specific area.
- Build a UVP that solves a problem and provides significant benefits to customers.
- Differentiate the business from competitors by offering a unique solution rather than competing solely on cost.

For an entrepreneur, navigating the terrain of business isn't merely about networking; it's about showcasing a tangible value proposition. It's about substantiating our worth through measurable outcomes, transcending mere acquaintanceship to forge enduring alliances grounded in mutual benefit and trust. Ultimately, it is this relentless commitment to delivering substantive value that sustains our journey and ensures our longevity in the dynamic landscape of entrepreneurship. However, not having a clear UVP can lead to a lack of direction, confusion in the market, and difficulty in attracting and retaining customers.

A UVP that resonates is one that aligns closely with the needs, wants, and challenges of your target market. Understanding your audience at this level is paramount in crafting a proposition that feels almost tailor-made.

Understanding the essence of a unique value proposition became crystal clear to me when I transitioned to European markets to spearhead business ventures for the organizations I had previously collaborated with. It was a paradigm shift; the Indian software company strategies that proved effective in the US or UK, such as cost-effectiveness or technological innovation, failed to yield results in continental Europe. The realization dawned upon me that the European market operated under distinct dynamics, necessitating a tailored approach.

Initially, navigating through this unfamiliar terrain was arduous. Despite our best efforts, success seemed elusive. It was then that we embarked on a 'journey of introspection,' a process of self-reflection and analysis, to unravel the underlying reasons behind our struggle. The crux of the matter lay in our positioning; what worked elsewhere simply didn't resonate here. The landscape of continental Europe demanded a unique perspective, one that mirrored its intricate business culture. This experience taught us the importance of understanding the market and its nuances in defining a UVP, as well as the potential pitfalls of not doing so.

Reflecting on my career trajectory, I gleaned a fundamental truth: differentiation is paramount in the realm of startups. To merely exist as a generalist amidst a sea of competitors is to fade into obscurity. The path to prominence lies in carving out a niche, becoming synonymous with excellence in a specific domain. This revelation spurred us to redefine our identity and craft a value proposition that would set us apart.

As we embarked on this transformative journey, we encountered inevitable obstacles. Financial constraints compelled us to engage in ancillary activities to sustain our endeavor. Yet, our unwavering commitment to refining our value proposition remained steadfast. Through perseverance and innovation, we birthed a proposition so distinctive that it garnered the attention of industry stalwarts, including Gartner.

In a marketplace saturated with generic solutions driven by cost, our emphasis on value proposition proved to be our ace in the hole. It wasn't merely about offering a product; it was about solving a problem in a way that conferred unparalleled advantages to our clientele. This strategic approach was instrumental in catapulting us to the forefront of the market, solidifying our foothold amidst stiff competition.

In retrospect, our journey underscores the pivotal role played by a well-defined value proposition in navigating the complexities of today's business landscape. It serves as a beacon of differentiation, illuminating the path to sustained success amidst the ever-shifting currents of the market.

Importance of Articulating Value Propositions

Tailoring Solutions to Specific Needs

I emphasize the importance of clearly articulating how their solution solves problems, simplifies processes, reduces costs, or speeds up processes. It's crucial to quantify these benefits to demonstrate return on investment (ROI) effectively.

Customizing Value Propositions

Each customer's needs are unique, requiring customized value propositions. It's essential to identify which aspects of the solution are most relevant to each customer and focus on articulating the ROI in those specific areas.

Conducting Research

Prior research on potential clients is critical. Understanding their vendor ecosystem, financial situation, growth objectives, and market performance allows businesses to tailor their value propositions effectively. This research not only demonstrates understanding but also positions the business as a strategic partner capable of delivering relevant solutions.

Market Research for Client Engagement

Engaging in detailed market research on identified target customers enhances credibility. It shows a commitment to understanding their business challenges and objectives, which resonates positively with decision-makers.

Takeaways

1. **Articulate Benefits Clearly**: Clearly outline how your solution solves problems, simplifies processes, reduces costs, or improves speed.
2. **Quantify ROI**: Quantify the benefits wherever possible to demonstrate tangible returns for the customer.
3. **Customize for Each Client**: Tailor the value proposition to address the specific needs and priorities of each client.
4. **Prioritize Research**: Conduct thorough research on potential clients to understand their business environment, challenges, and growth opportunities.
5. **Demonstrate Understanding**: Use market research findings to show a deep understanding of the client's situation and needs, enhancing credibility and trust.

Action Items

- **Articulate Value Propositions**: Ensure each benefit of the solution is clearly articulated.
- **Quantify Benefits**: Quantify ROI and value wherever possible to substantiate claims.
- **Customize Messaging**: Tailor value propositions to address specific client needs and priorities.
- **Conduct Research**: Invest time in thorough research on potential clients to understand their business context and challenges.

- **Enhance Credibility**: Use market research insights to demonstrate a deep understanding of the client's situation, fostering trust and credibility in engagements.

As an entrepreneur, your enthusiasm should be a beacon, infusing the team with a similar zeal. It's not just about leading; it's about inspiring, motivating, and fostering a culture of passion and dedication. Your engagement with team members, your ability to keep them in good humor, and your alignment of their efforts with market dynamics and industry trends are crucial components of effective leadership. Remember, your leadership has a direct impact on team morale and their sense of empowerment and responsibility.

Transparency and consistency are paramount. It's not enough to simply dictate; one must lead by example. Demonstrating discipline, integrity, and a commitment to the shared vision sets the tone for the entire organization. When leaders walk the talk, it instills confidence and trust within the team.

Collaboration is not just a key; it's THE key. Success isn't achieved in isolation; it's a collective endeavor. Regularly reviewing goals, plans, and progress in consultation with the team ensures alignment and fosters a sense of ownership and accountability. Addressing challenges together cultivates resilience and strengthens bonds, leading to a more cohesive and productive team. Remember, it's the unity and motivation that collaboration brings that drives success.

Building a unique value proposition is foundational. It's about identifying opportunities, understanding market trends, and addressing common pain points potential customers face. Thorough research is essential to ensure that our solutions resonate with the market and offer genuine value.

Furthermore, creating an inclusive and positive work environment is imperative. Small gestures, such as branding items or leveraging social media for visibility, can go a long way in fostering a sense of belonging and pride among team members. Employees who feel valued and appreciated are more likely to be engaged, productive, and committed to the organization's success.

Ultimately, success lies in creating a workplace where individuals are empowered to do their best work, where innovation thrives, and where everyone shares in the collective journey towards achieving our goals. By prioritizing both the development of a compelling value proposition and the cultivation of a supportive and inspiring workplace culture, we can lay the foundation for sustainable growth and long-term success.

Solving Business Problems

A successful unique value proposition must address specific business challenges, such as high costs, information accessibility issues, interoperability problems, or operational inefficiencies. These issues directly impact financial outcomes and operational effectiveness.

Demonstrating Tangible Value

It's crucial to link the value proposition directly to how it benefits the business, whether by saving costs, increasing sales, or enhancing operational efficiency. They cite an example where their solution achieved a significant 32% budget savings for a customer, demonstrating the tangible impact of their approach.

Building Trust through Value Delivery

Building trust with customers hinges on consistently delivering sustainable solutions that address their ongoing business challenges. This approach not only validates the value proposition but also establishes credibility and fosters long-term relationships.

Focus on Sustainable Solutions

Success is rooted in providing sustainable solutions rather than relying solely on personal connections. Delivering measurable value is essential for maintaining business sustainability and attracting new customers based on demonstrated success.

Takeaways

1. **Problem-Solving Value Proposition**: Ensure your value proposition directly addresses specific business problems that impact finances or operations.
2. **Quantify Benefits**: Use real-world examples and case studies to quantify and demonstrate the tangible value and cost savings your solution can provide.
3. **Build Trust**: Focus on continuously delivering sustainable solutions that meet evolving business challenges, thereby building trust and credibility.
4. **Value Over Relationships**: While relationships are important, sustainable business success relies on delivering tangible value through effective solutions.

Action Items

- **Develop Clear Value Propositions**: Tailor your value proposition to solve critical business problems faced by potential customers.
- **Demonstrate Tangible Benefits**: Quantify and showcase how your solution can save costs, increase sales, or enhance operations.
- **Build Long-Term Relationships**: Focus on delivering ongoing value to build trust and credibility with customers.
- **Emphasize Value Delivery**: Highlight the sustainability and effectiveness of your solutions rather than relying solely on personal connections.

This approach ensures that your business proposition resonates with potential clients by addressing their immediate needs and showcasing measurable benefits.

Gaining Trust Through Authenticity

Authenticity shouldn't just be a buzzword; it's the bedrock of your relationship with your customers. Your Unique Value Proposition (UVP) should be a true reflection of what you believe and what you can deliver. It encompasses your core values and the genuine commitment you bring to your business. When your UVP is authentic, it resonates deeply with your audience, building trust and fostering long-term loyalty. By aligning your UVP with your brand's true essence, you create a compelling narrative that not only attracts customers but also keeps them engaged and satisfied.

Case Study: Red Rabbit

Struggle and Early Days

Red Rabbit was founded by Rhys Powell in 2005 with a mission to provide healthy meals to schoolchildren in New York City. Powell's inspiration for the company stemmed from his observation of the poor quality of food served in schools. Recognizing the long-term impact of nutrition on children's health and academic performance, Powell set out to make a difference. However, the journey was fraught with numerous challenges and failures that nearly derailed the company before it could find its footing.

One of the primary hurdles was skepticism from schools and parents. Convincing them to switch from traditional, often less nutritious options to healthier meals was no easy task. Many doubted the feasibility of providing nutritious food that children would actually enjoy eating. Additionally, the logistical challenges of preparing and delivering thousands of meals daily presented a significant obstacle. Powell had to establish a supply chain that could ensure fresh, locally sourced ingredients while maintaining high standards of quality and safety.

Initially, the company struggled with scaling its operations. There were instances of logistical mishaps, such as late deliveries and incorrect meal orders, which tarnished Red Rabbit's reputation in its early days. Financial instability also loomed large as the company faced high operational costs and slim margins. These challenges led to periods of significant stress for Powell and his team, with doubts about the sustainability of their business model.

Failures and Setbacks

Several notable setbacks marked the road to success for Red Rabbit:

1. **Skepticism and Resistance**: Many schools and parents were resistant to changing their meal providers, preferring the familiar over the new. This resistance led to slow initial adoption rates and limited revenue.
2. **Operational Challenges**: The logistics of preparing and delivering thousands of fresh meals daily proved daunting. Early on, Red Rabbit faced numerous operational issues, including delays, inaccuracies in orders, and spoilage of ingredients.
3. **Financial Strain**: High costs associated with sourcing quality ingredients, coupled with the need for specialized kitchen facilities and staff, placed significant financial strain on the company. There were times when cash flow issues threatened the very existence of Red Rabbit.
4. **Quality Control**: Ensuring consistent quality across all meals was another major challenge. Initial hiccups in maintaining high standards led to dissatisfaction among some schools and parents, further complicating efforts to expand the business.

Rising from the Ashes: The Phoenix Moment

Despite these daunting challenges, Red Rabbit's commitment to its mission of providing nutritious meals never wavered. Rhys Powell and his team undertook several strategic measures to turn the tide and rise from the ashes like a phoenix.

1. **Revamping Operations**: Red Rabbit overhauled its logistics and operations. They invested in better technology and systems to track orders, manage inventory, and streamline delivery processes. This investment paid off by reducing errors and improving efficiency.
2. **Building Trust**: The company worked diligently to build trust with schools and parents. They held tasting events, provided transparency about their sourcing practices, and engaged with the community to highlight the benefits of their meals. This outreach helped overcome skepticism and build a loyal customer base.
3. **Focus on Quality**: Red Rabbit doubled down on its commitment to quality. They sourced even better ingredients, hired skilled chefs, and implemented rigorous quality control measures. Ensuring that every meal was nutritious and delicious became a non-negotiable standard.
4. **Financial Prudence**: Powell secured additional funding from investors who believed in the company's mission. This financial support allowed Red Rabbit to stabilize its cash flow and invest in necessary infrastructure improvements. They also renegotiated supplier contracts to achieve better pricing without compromising on quality.
5. **Innovation and Adaptation**: Red Rabbit continuously adapted its menu based on feedback from students and schools. They introduced new dishes that catered to children's tastes while maintaining nutritional value. This adaptability kept their offerings fresh and appealing.
6. **Community and Advocacy**: The company actively participated in advocacy for better school nutrition policies. By aligning itself with broader movements for healthier school meals, Red Rabbit

positioned itself as a leader in the space and garnered additional support and recognition.

Gaining Trust Through Authenticity

A critical factor in Red Rabbit's success was its ability to gain trust through authenticity. From the beginning, Powell emphasized transparency and honesty in every aspect of the business. This authentic approach resonated deeply with schools, parents, and students, helping to build a loyal customer base.

1. **Transparent Practices**: Red Rabbit made its sourcing practices transparent, showcasing the local farms and suppliers they partnered with. This openness built trust and demonstrated their commitment to quality and sustainability.
2. **Engaging the Community**: Red Rabbit engaged directly with the community through events, workshops, and school visits. By educating parents and school staff about the importance of nutrition and how their meals were prepared, they fostered a sense of community and trust.
3. **Consistent Values**: The company's values of health, quality, and sustainability were consistently reflected in its actions and communications. This consistency reassured customers that Red Rabbit was genuinely committed to its mission.
4. **Personalized Service**: Red Rabbit took the time to understand the unique needs and preferences of each school they served. This personalized approach made schools feel valued and built strong, lasting relationships.

Success and Growth

These strategic efforts paid off. Red Rabbit began to see significant improvements in their operations and customer satisfaction. Schools and parents who had initially been skeptical became ardent supporters, impressed by the quality and consistency of the meals. As word spread, more schools signed up for Red Rabbit's services.

The company expanded its services to over 200 schools and childcare centers, proving that a focus on quality and nutrition can drive success in the competitive food service industry. Red Rabbit's growth can be attributed to several key factors:

1. **Quality and Nutrition**: By prioritizing fresh, locally sourced ingredients, Red Rabbit ensured that their meals were not only healthy **but** also delicious. This commitment to quality sets them apart from other food service providers.
2. **Engagement and Education**: Red Rabbit actively engaged with schools and parents to educate them about the importance of nutrition. By involving them in the process, the company built a community of advocates who supported their mission.
3. **Adaptability and Innovation**: Red Rabbit continuously adapted their menu based on feedback from students and schools. This willingness to innovate and improve helped them stay relevant and meet the evolving needs of their customers.
4. **Sustainability and Social Responsibility**: Red Rabbit's focus on using locally sourced ingredients also promoted sustainability. This approach not only supported local farmers but also resonated with the growing demand for environmentally conscious practices.

Lessons from Red Rabbit's Journey

Red Rabbit's journey from a struggling startup facing skepticism to a successful company serving over 200 schools is a testament to the power of resilience, innovation, and a clear vision. Rhys Powell's determination to improve school nutrition and his ability to navigate the logistical challenges paved the way for Red Rabbit's success.

The key takeaways from Red Rabbit's success include:

- **Identify a Meaningful Problem**: Powell's observation of poor school food quality led to the creation of Red Rabbit. Identifying a meaningful problem that resonates with a wide audience can be the foundation of a successful business.
- **Commit to Quality**: Red Rabbit's focus on quality and nutrition sets them apart from competitors. Ensuring high standards can build trust and loyalty among customers.
- **Engage with Stakeholders**: Building relationships with schools, parents, and students helped Red Rabbit gain support and address concerns. Engaging with stakeholders can provide valuable insights and foster a sense of community.
- **Adapt and Innovate**: Red Rabbit's ability to adapt their menu and innovate based on feedback was crucial to their success. Staying flexible and responsive to customer needs can drive continuous improvement and growth.
- **Resilience in the Face of Failure**: Red Rabbit's story shows that setbacks and failures are part of the entrepreneurial journey. By learning from these experiences and persisting through challenges, it's possible to emerge stronger and more successful.
- **Gaining Trust Through Authenticity**: Red Rabbit's authentic approach to business practices, community engagement, and consistent values helped build a loyal customer base. Authenticity and transparency can significantly enhance trust and loyalty among customers.

Red Rabbit's story demonstrates that entrepreneurial success is achievable through a clear mission, dedication to quality, and the ability to overcome challenges. It serves as an inspiring example for aspiring entrepreneurs, showing that with the right approach, it is possible to make a significant impact and achieve sustainable growth.

PURSUIT OF AN IDENTITY

This is your call for action: Take the first step towards defining your UVP by listing your core strengths and passions and how they meet a specific market need. Craft a preliminary UVP statement and test it out with potential customers for feedback. Remember, your UVP is a living part of your business, evolving as you grow.

With your unique value proposition shining bright and guiding customers to your door, it's time to build on that foundation. In the next chapter, "Building Your Niche and Market Strategy," we'll dive into how to position your business to reach those who need your unique value the most. Your UVP is the beacon; now, let's chart the course to navigate the market waters successfully.

Chapter 5

BUILDING YOUR NICHE AND MARKET STRATEGY

"The key to success is to find a niche and fill it."

— **Warren Buffett**

In the vast market ecosystem, finding your niche is like discovering a fertile valley in the wilderness. This valley is a place where your business can not only survive but thrive, much like a fertile valley that provides the perfect conditions for crops to grow. This chapter is about charting the map to that valley, understanding the terrain, and planting your flag to claim your unique space. A well-defined niche and a strategic market approach are not just essential; they are the key to carving out a successful space for your business in a crowded marketplace. By identifying your niche, understanding your target audience, and developing a market strategy, you can navigate the market's complexities and lay a solid foundation for long-term success. This is your path to growth and sustainability, empowering you to take control of your business's destiny.

The journey begins with keen observation and research to uncover unmet needs within the market. By pinpointing specific gaps, you can develop tailored solutions that address these needs, setting your business apart from the competition. This initial focus on a specialized area not only helps you stand out but also allows you to build credibility and expertise. Understanding your target audience is not just crucial; it's a way to make them feel valued and integral to your business strategy, fostering a sense of belonging and loyalty.

As you refine your offerings and demonstrate their effectiveness through real-world applications, you will gain the confidence of key customers. Securing a major enterprise customer can serve as a powerful launchpad, validating your approach and providing a strong foundation for further expansion. This achievement is not just a milestone; it's a source of inspiration and motivation that fuels your ambition to build a broader portfolio and gradually scale your business by leveraging these success stories.

Building a Niche Market Strategy

Importance of Specialization

The criticality of developing a niche or specialized market strategy, particularly for small startups or companies launching without extensive financial backing. They stress that entering a crowded market requires a specific and focused approach to differentiate oneself effectively.

Identifying Market Gaps

It's crucial to identify gaps in the market or industry segment where potential solutions can address specific problems or unmet needs. This approach involves careful observation and research into existing dominant players, their capabilities, and the opportunities for differentiation.

Demonstration of Capability

Starting as a niche provider allows for the demonstration of capabilities through focused solutions that solve specific problems. Building initial solutions or prototypes that showcase how the business can effectively fill identified gaps in the market is essential.

Importance of Enterprise Customers

Engaging with large enterprise customers early on can be pivotal. These customers not only validate the solution but also provide a launchpad for credibility and further market penetration. By being proactive and engaging with these clients, you can build trust and demonstrate value through early successes, which is crucial for long-term business growth.

Focus on Sustainable Growth

While acknowledging the allure of scaling quickly, one can argue that maintaining a specialized focus often leads to sustainable growth. Unlike more generalized approaches that can lead to increased competition and limited differentiation, specialization allows for deeper market penetration and continued innovation.

1. **Niche Strategy**: Start with a specialized market strategy to effectively compete in a crowded marketplace.
2. **Identify Market Gaps**: Conduct thorough research to identify gaps where your business can provide unique solutions.
3. **Demonstrate Capabilities**: Build initial solutions or prototypes to showcase your ability to solve specific business challenges.
4. **Enterprise Validation**: Early engagement with enterprise customers can provide credibility and serve as a springboard for broader market acceptance.
5. **Sustainable Growth**: Emphasize sustainable growth over rapid scaling by focusing on niche specialization and continuous innovation.

Actionable Insights

- **Research and Observation**: Invest time in understanding market dynamics, identifying gaps, and studying incumbent players.
- **Prototype Development**: Develop prototypes or initial solutions that demonstrate your capability to solve specific business problems.
- **Enterprise Engagement**: Target early engagement with large enterprise customers to validate solutions and build credibility.
- **Specialization Over Generalization**: Prioritize specialization to differentiate from competitors and foster sustainable business growth.

Whether you are a startup or an established business looking to innovate, the principles outlined here will provide the tools needed to thrive in a competitive landscape. My experience underscores the importance of strategic entry into competitive markets through specialization and niche focus. By focusing on solving specific business problems and demonstrating value early on, startups can establish a strong foundation for growth and expansion into broader market segments.

When embarking on a small startup, resources are often limited, and a large-scale launch with substantial financial backing may not be feasible. However, a focused approach is not only essential but also empowering. Specializing in a niche area allows you to concentrate your limited resources on becoming an expert in a specific field. This expertise helps you stand out in a crowded market where many businesses offer various products or services. You can effectively differentiate yourself from competitors by identifying and targeting a specific market need. This strategy leverages your unique strengths and ensures that you address unmet needs, increasing the likelihood of success.

Building Your Niche and Market Strategy

Defining Your Unique Value Proposition

Your unique value proposition (UVP) is vital as the cornerstone of your niche market strategy. It's not just about having a unique offering but about demonstrating its value through tangible footprints of success. This is crucial for gaining traction in the market and should be a motivating factor for your business strategy.

Go-to-Market Strategies

- **Partner Ecosystem**: Collaborate with existing partners in the ecosystem to leverage their networks to sell your services or solutions.

- **Direct Engagement**: Consider direct engagement with customers to build relationships and demonstrate your value proposition firsthand.
- **System Integration**: Alternatively, focus on becoming a system integrator to embed your solutions into broader offerings.

The choice between these strategies depends on available resources and strategic goals, whether it's independent growth, attracting investment, or scaling for exit.

Strategic Clarity for Entrepreneurs

I advise entrepreneurs to define their niche clearly and align their growth plans with their long-term vision. This includes:

- **Understanding Strengths**: Recognize personal strengths as an entrepreneur, such as innovation and solution-building, versus skills needed for scaling a large organization.
- **Exit Strategy**: Define exit criteria, whether it's scaling to a certain revenue level, going public, or positioning the business for acquisition.

Importance of Vision and Planning

Entrepreneurs must outline a clear three-year plan that aligns with their strengths and long-term goals. This clarity guides immediate strategies and shapes future growth and potential exit strategies.

Takeaways

1. **UVP as Foundation**: Your unique value proposition should be clearly defined and demonstrated through successful implementations.

2. **Diverse Go-to-Market Strategies**: Choose from partnering with ecosystems, direct engagement with customers, or system integration based on your resources and strategic objectives.
3. **Entrepreneurial Clarity**: Understand your strengths and long-term goals to define a scalable path forward, including potential exit strategies.

Actionable Insights

- **Define Your UVP**: Clearly articulate how your solution addresses market needs and provides unique benefits.
- **Choose Strategic Partnerships**: Evaluate the benefits of partnering with existing ecosystems versus direct customer engagement or becoming a system integrator.
- **Plan for Growth**: Develop a clear three-year plan that outlines growth milestones and aligns with your entrepreneurial strengths and vision.

These insights underscore the empowering process of defining and demonstrating a unique value proposition within a niche market strategy. By aligning go-to-market approaches with personal strengths and long-term goals, entrepreneurs can effectively position their ventures for sustainable growth and strategic success, feeling inspired and motivated by their own potential.

To succeed, keen observation and research are necessary to identify unmet needs or gaps within a market. By understanding these gaps, you can develop solutions that directly address them, creating a new market or filling an existing void. This process instills a sense of pride and confidence in your ability to create and innovate, leading to a strong foundation for further expansion.

Understanding the competitive landscape is crucial. Knowing what dominant players offer allows you to identify areas where they may be lacking or where you can provide a unique value proposition. Differentiation is key to standing out. By developing a robust solution and demonstrating its effectiveness, you can validate and refine your approach based on real-world feedback, which includes customer reviews, market trends, and industry insights. This hands-on experience helps create a solution that meets market needs and surpasses existing offerings in certain aspects.

Demonstrating your solution through real business cases is an effective way to show its practical value. By selecting critical cases and creating detailed workflows, you can illustrate your solution's tangible benefits and efficiency. This method helps potential customers visualize how your product can address their specific needs. In my experience, presenting these cases to potential clients significantly increases their interest and confidence in your offering. Conducting thorough research to identify gaps and engaging with potential large customers early on can secure key partnerships and validate your business model. Starting with a major enterprise customer provides a solid foundation and credibility.

Securing a large enterprise customer base can significantly boost your business. This customer acts as a validation of your solution's effectiveness and reliability. As they begin to see the value you provide, they are likely to deepen their engagement with your company. Solving their problems effectively can lead to a strong, ongoing relationship and further business opportunities. Demonstrating a few successful business cases is essential to gaining initial confidence. Building a strong foundation of success stories through direct engagement with key customers helps create a track record of reliability. Once established, these success stories can be leveraged in broader marketing efforts, making indirect sales more effective.

By following a niche strategy, we built strong credibility in the market. Over time, this approach allowed us to expand our portfolio, particularly in the identity management space. Our solutions gained recognition, as evidenced by mentions in analyst reports, which further boosted our visibility and reputation. This visibility helped us grow from a local to a global presence, extending our reach to the US, Europe, and Asia Pacific. The key to this growth was our ability to solve specific problems that others overlooked, demonstrating the importance of being observant and dedicated to addressing market needs effectively.

European companies often focus on their core competencies without broadening their scope significantly. This contrasts with the approach of many Indian companies, which tend to expand rapidly but sometimes fail due to intense competition. My experience in Europe underscored the value of a niche strategy. We applied this approach by initially focusing on specialized areas and gradually expanding our portfolio. Even when entering new enterprises with significant competition, we maintained our niche strategy to solve specific problems. This approach ensures that customers receive highly tailored solutions, making them more likely to engage with us comprehensively. For startups, identifying and focusing on a niche is critical for building a sustainable and competitive business model.

Drawing from my experience, building a niche and market strategy is essential for sustained success. Many specialized companies in Europe exemplify how focusing on core competencies can lead to thriving businesses. In contrast, the generalist approach seen in many Indian companies often fails due to the high level of competition. Our growth and success were driven by focusing on niche markets and solving specific problems. This approach allowed us to build expertise, credibility, and a strong market presence. Specialization and observance are crucial in identifying opportunities and developing solutions that address unmet needs, leading to long-term growth and competitive advantage.

Sara Blakely's journey to success with **Spanx** is a quintessential story of entrepreneurial innovation in a niche market. Blakely, who had no formal background in fashion or textiles, stumbled upon her business idea out of personal frustration. While getting ready for a party, she wanted a smooth look under white pants but couldn't find any satisfactory undergarment solution. She decided to cut the feet off her control top pantyhose, which worked perfectly. Recognizing a gap in the market, she spent her savings of $5,000 to develop her prototype.

Blakely faced numerous rejections from hosiery mills, but her persistence paid off when one mill owner finally agreed to manufacture her product. She patented her design and began selling Spanx from her apartment. Blakely's unique approach to marketing—personally demonstrating the product in stores and securing a spot on Oprah Winfrey's show—catapulted Spanx to national fame.

By focusing on shapewear, a previously underdeveloped niche in women's fashion, Blakely was able to build a billion-dollar business. Spanx expanded its product line to include leggings, swimwear, and men's underwear, all while maintaining a reputation for comfort and innovation. Blakely's story highlights the power of identifying and capitalizing on niche markets, as well as the importance of perseverance and hands-on marketing.

A great example of a historical niche triumph in the marketplace is that of the luxury watchmaking brand **Rolex**. **Rolex** was founded in 1905 by **Hans Wilsdorf** and **Alfred Davis** in London. Initially, they imported Swiss movements and placed them in quality cases to create reliable timepieces. Wilsdorf saw an opportunity to differentiate Rolex from other watchmakers by focusing on precision and durability—key aspects that would appeal to a niche market of professionals who required reliable timekeeping.

In 1910, Rolex became the first wristwatch to receive the Swiss Certificate of Chronometric Precision, awarded by the Official Watch Rating Centre in Bienne. This focus on precision continued with the development of the first waterproof wristwatch, the Rolex Oyster, in 1926. The Oyster case featured a hermetically sealed design, protecting the movement from dust and water, which was a groundbreaking innovation at the time.

Rolex further cemented its reputation for durability with the introduction of the Perpetual movement in 1931, the first self-winding mechanism with a rotor. This development ensured that the watch remained consistently wound and accurate with the movement of the wearer's wrist. By consistently targeting a niche market that valued precision, reliability, and innovation, Rolex built a brand synonymous with luxury and excellence.

Rolex's niche focus allowed it to command a premium price and develop a loyal customer base. Their watches became a symbol of success and prestige, worn by explorers, athletes, and professionals in demanding environments. This strategic focus on a specific market segment enabled Rolex to thrive and become one of the most recognized and respected brands in the world.

Another entrepreneur cum author whose journey resonates with me is **Seth Godin**. Godin, a prolific author, dot com entrepreneur, and marketing guru, is known for his emphasis on the importance of being remarkable in niche markets. In "Purple Cow: Transform Your Business by Being Remarkable," Godin argues that in a crowded marketplace, the only way to stand out is to create something truly unique – a "purple cow" in a field of brown cows.

Godin's analysis showcases the unique strategies of successful brands. For instance, Starbucks redefined the coffee experience by not merely selling coffee but by creating a "third place" – a space between home and work – where people could unwind with premium coffee beverages. This innovative approach set Starbucks apart from traditional coffee shops and fast-food chains, enabling it to dominate the specialty coffee niche.

Similarly, Godin underscores Apple's triumph through its unwavering focus on innovative technology and exceptional design, which resonates with a niche market of creative professionals and tech enthusiasts. Apple's dedication to this niche market, coupled with its ability to consistently innovate and produce aesthetically pleasing products, fostered a loyal customer base and propelled the company to global prominence.

Godin's insights underline the significance of businesses understanding and deeply engaging with their niche audience. He advises businesses to concentrate on what sets them apart and to exploit that uniqueness to foster strong connections with their target market. By being extraordinary and catering to a specific audience's needs, businesses can achieve substantial success even in competitive markets. Godin's work offers a roadmap for businesses aiming to carve out and dominate their own niches.

Takeaways

1. **Focused Resource Use:** Niche marketing allows for a more focused and effective use of resources. By targeting a specific segment of the market, businesses can allocate their marketing, production, and operational resources more efficiently. This concentration enables higher productivity and better results compared to a broader, more generalized approach.
2. **Target Audience Understanding:** Identifying and understanding your niche and target audience is crucial for building a strong marketing strategy. By honing in on a specific group of consumers, businesses can gain deeper insights into their needs, preferences, and behaviors. This understanding allows for the creation of tailored products, services, and marketing messages that resonate more strongly with the target audience.
3. **Market Differentiation:** A well-defined niche can help your business stand out in a crowded market. By focusing on a specific area, businesses can develop unique selling propositions (USPs) that set them apart from competitors. This differentiation can

attract a loyal customer base that values the specialized products or services offered.
4. **Credibility and Trust:** Specializing in a niche builds credibility and fosters customer trust. When a business consistently delivers high-quality, specialized products or services, it establishes itself as an expert in that field. This expertise builds customer confidence and loyalty, as customers are more likely to trust a specialist over a generalist.
5. **Avoiding Dilution:** Spreading your efforts too thin can dilute your brand and weaken your market position. By trying to appeal to everyone, businesses risk becoming mediocre in multiple areas instead of excelling in one. A focused niche strategy helps maintain a strong, clear brand identity, ensuring that efforts are concentrated on delivering exceptional value to a specific group of customers.

Start today by taking a deep dive into your business's strengths, market needs, and potential niches. Here are the steps to get started:

1. **Assess Your Strengths:** Evaluate what your business does best. Identify the unique skills, expertise, and resources that set your business apart.
2. **Conduct Market Research:** Investigate the market to identify gaps and unmet needs. Look for areas where your strengths can address specific problems or desires.
3. **Define Your Niche:** Based on your strengths and market research, pinpoint a specific niche where your business can thrive. Ensure that this niche is large enough to be profitable but focused enough to allow for specialization.
4. **Engage with Your Target Audience:** Connect with potential customers within your niche to gather feedback and refine your approach. Use surveys, interviews, and social media interactions to understand their needs and preferences better.
5. **Develop a Tailored Marketing Strategy:** Craft a marketing strategy that speaks directly to your niche audience. Use targeted

messaging, personalized campaigns, and relevant content to engage and attract your ideal customers.

Having identified your fertile valley and planted your flag, it's time to cultivate the land. You've taken the crucial first steps in carving out your niche and laying the foundation for your business. Now, the next phase is about nurturing and growing your relationship with your niche market.

In the next chapter, "Delivering Exceptional Value to Customers," we'll delve into strategies for building and maintaining strong connections with your target audience. We'll explore how to consistently deliver unmatched value, create memorable customer experiences, and ensure the longevity and prosperity of your business in its chosen terrain. By focusing on delivering exceptional value, you will not only retain your current customers but also attract new ones, securing a robust position in your niche market.

Chapter 6

DELIVERING EXCEPTIONAL VALUE TO CUSTOMERS

"Quality in a service or product is not what you put into it. It is what the client or customer gets out of it."

— **Peter Drucker**

Imagine a world where every customer interaction with your business leaves them feeling valued, understood, and delighted. This isn't a utopian fantasy; it's the cornerstone of businesses that thrive and create lasting impacts. This chapter is about making that vision a reality by focusing on delivering exceptional value to your customers.

The essence of a successful business lies not just in the products or services it offers but in the value it delivers to its customers. Exceptional customer value goes beyond transactions; it's about creating meaningful experiences that foster loyalty, advocacy, and sustained growth. This chapter explores how to understand and anticipate customer needs, personalize experiences, and ensure continuous improvement in your value delivery.

Customer satisfaction should be a frequent occurrence, not a rare event. To illustrate this, consider a game of chess between grandmasters. You know the game can be optimized with promotions, just like a business can be improved with customer feedback.

The idea is to make the game easier by promoting as many pawns as possible to queens, rooks, or knights. However, sometimes sacrifices need to be made. In the end, you might end up with only a single or no promotion, which is what the viewer might expect. This is similar to companies like Windows and Apple, whose inspiring success stories should ignite a sense of optimism and motivate us with their journey of collecting user feedback.

This feedback, often overlooked or circumnavigated by users, is a valuable database of insights that can significantly enhance our system. Many companies, including ours, follow this feedback routine, making our systems more user-friendly. This helps in the whole notion of research and development and makes the updates we work on more appealing to the new market we intend to open to.

This is like a game of chess where you make an adjustment based on your opponent's feedback on the move. The difference is that you compete with the consumer base's expectations and your competitors' actions. You are meant to keep in touch with the reality of your company's image and what people would like to expect from it. If you do not engage with the customers, you might take leaps too big to meet your customer base, which could lead to over-expenditure. This could work in favor of your company if the customer base is established at a scale for a suitable return on investment.

However, if you make too many improvements without considering your customer's response, you might overshoot your target. This could lead to a struggle to recover that margin on a move that was taken without an inventory of your customer response. The idea is to gauge your position in the market. This can be made apparent if you have healthy correspondence with the customers.

Healthy customer communication is not just a way to provide necessary service but a means to empower our customers. This is evident in Nike's inspiring journey. Nike was primarily known for producing running and track shoes, but to make a mark in the basketball market, they had to create a product that would fill in the gaps left by the competitors.

They did this by signing an up-and-coming star in the sport and gathering enough feedback to base the requirements of an athlete in the field. For instance, they learned that basketball players needed shoes with better ankle support and cushioning.

This led to the adjustments required by the prospective users of the product. In the process, it became a step toward carving a spot in the market. They built a brand through their partnership with the athlete and became the frontrunner in the field. This data was applied across the brand in the basketball department.

Over time, the brand became synonymous with the basketball equipment department. They solidified their position by doing more hands-on research and development. What came out of it was a masterpiece that improved with every update to the shoe. This also meant the customer would need more room to find the product cumbersome. Additionally, making the process of the shoes appeal to a hands-on one made it easier to relate to the connection between the maker and the product.

The inspiring journey of Nike's involvement of customers in their product development should excite us about the potential of our customer base in shaping our future. It also underscores the importance of healthy customer communication in fostering brand loyalty. By actively listening to our customers and incorporating their feedback into our products and services, we can build a strong and loyal customer base, a strategy we can confidently adopt to strengthen customer relationships.

The idea is that you can be more than just a producer of a product or a provider of a service; you can add to the relationship between you and your customer. In addition, you can form a community around your product. This means the customers feel like they're a part of the company's journey.

Now, some companies may seem like they are beyond their fanbase or like there's a lack thereof. Like the Google Pay service by Google, it looks like there's a customer base because of the need for the application.

However, even these sub-brands of the bigger companies are involved in improving the user experience by requesting the user to fill out a feedback form. This could help in the long run if there are alternatives to your company's service. You have a likelihood of retaining the original user base. This is a valuable asset. This means that finances are coming in at a sturdy rate, providing a stable income for the company. The inspiring journey of involving customers in shaping our future should excite us about the potential impact they can have on our company's success.

The idea is to avoid hitting a sense of stagnancy in your impact on the base audience of your product. This will lead to the image of being bored or annoyed when interacting with many of the big names in the market and become distant memories. For example, it has been a while since you'd last heard of Kodak. Kodak has fallen from its claim to fame and domination of the market for a while now because of its strange fear of giving in to changing times. This also shows how disconnected from the world outside their element they were. Most consumers switched to the new system because of convenience in the matter of a heartbeat. This can easily signify that many inconveniences were already present in the product.

Understanding Customer Needs

Create a Buyer's Persona: A buyer's persona is a fictional yet detailed profile representation of your ideal customer based on market research and real data about your existing customers. It helps you understand your customers better, making it easy to gauge the marketing concepts you can follow. A trend is always set based on the likes and dislikes of the community you approach with a product. This is something that can make a good appeal to the user base. To add to this is the idea that you need to keep updating since trends keep updating.

A flaw with the bigger competitors is that they tend to target the more mainstream trends when they try to make an effort. This means that you can pay attention to a finer focused margin of the market and give an image that the brand you're building is keeping up with the trends. This will help you be even more appealing to your current users and help create a community around that, expanding to a wider audience. The urgency of understanding customer needs cannot be overstated. It is the key to staying relevant and competitive in the market.

Seek Feedback from Customers: A method similar to the example of Nike is to use a single point of reference, such as a popular customer or a well-known industry expert, to find a more proficient manner to improve your product. This could have you appeal to all the issues in the field and resolve the matter. This valid system can be more hands-on in the processes, making it efficient.

However, the flaw of the approach is the assumption that everyone has the same needs as the single point of reference you're using. This would mean that even though you're approaching the issue of participating in a certain task or action. It might alienate some parts of the community that wouldn't have a similar preference. Another way to attain a sense of feedback is by sending feedback forms to gauge the necessary changes to improve the service experience.

This would include a comprehensive list of issues to fix. However, this approach also has a few drawbacks, such as that it could seem needy and mundane in many cases. This is because many companies implement similar strategies to make their product more optimal. A lot of times, this has resulted in users ignoring the process. Adding to the issue is the inclusion of anonymity to the user, which makes the responses filled with joke replies that can be useless.

Genuine replies can provide great insight into improving the product. However, challenging established companies can be tricky since some companies are built so that they sign established members in the field. This works more advantageously since these members would use the product more extensively to obtain the most of the product. This would help pinpoint the precise point of issue with the product.

Observing the market: Observing the market is also a wise strategy for making a mark. The bigger companies often hold back in implementing new solutions in anticipation of another company doing so. If they are successful, they adopt the method to reduce any loss in finance or trust of the board members. A simple example is the crash of Carvana, which helped many car manufacturers decide what not to do.

You can learn much about the market by taking a backseat approach, which means observing the actions and strategies of other companies without directly participating. This approach allows you to learn from the successes and failures of others without the risk and cost of direct participation. Since many companies tend to act recklessly, it is easy to know why a company failed. This approach has often been used with legacy brands in the public domain for a long time.

For example, Mitsubishi has been following the system of observing markets, and it is one of the best examples from which to learn. The company initially started as a shipping company. However, as a company, it discovered that there was profit in the coal business based on its demand. This was when it got into the coal mining industry by acquiring the Takashima Coal Mine, which cut down the spending on coal to fuel its ships.

They further expanded to shipbuilding, and they acquired the Nagasaki Shipyard. From this, they grew into a conglomerate. With this concept, they would expand to different markets based on market observation. The expansion kept up with the market demand as the need for the hour dictated, making them stable. This meant they could expand to ventures without fear of losing significantly; however, many of their endeavors have maintained consistent returns.

Delivering Exceptional Value to Customers

It emphasizes the significance of delivering exceptional value to customers, particularly as a niche player in the market. Here are the key insights:

Importance of Niche Expertise

- **Critical Problem Solving**: Being a niche player allows you to address critical aspects of solutions that larger vendors may overlook or not specialize in. This capability often resonates strongly with customers who struggle to find appropriate vendors.
- **Perceived Value**: Even if the solution's impact might seem insignificant in some contexts, the ability to solve a unique problem effectively garners significant attention and perceived value from customers.

Strategic Expansion

- **Scaling Strategy**: As you expand beyond your initial niche, it's crucial to plan meticulously to ensure the continued delivery of exceptional value. This involves not only maintaining but enhancing the value proposition compared to larger incumbents.
- **Example of Scale**: In my own startup experience, we focused on integrating subsystems for large enterprises, avoiding SMEs to maximize the value from each engagement. This approach allowed them to scale efficiently and cater to the complex needs of large enterprise customers.

Operational Excellence

- **Technical and Management Competency**: Beyond technical expertise, strong program management, and operational planning are essential, especially for large-scale implementations across multiple geographies and time zones.
- **Customer Confidence**: Building customer confidence is critical for a small company. This is achieved through

meticulous planning, exceeding expectations, and demonstrating continuous improvement in service delivery.

Long-term Customer Relationships

Sustainability: Small companies excel in delivering personalized attention and maintaining high standards of service, which can be challenging for larger organizations. This personalized approach fosters long-term customer relationships and opens doors for new opportunities.

Strategic Insights

- **Planning and Execution**: Detailed planning, regular customer communication, and consistent delivery beyond expectations are fundamental to success.
- **Market Differentiation**: By consistently solving unique problems and exceeding customer expectations, small companies can differentiate themselves from larger competitors and build a reputation for excellence.

These experiences underscore the power of niche expertise, meticulous planning, and exceptional delivery in establishing and sustaining a successful business. Small companies can survive and thrive in competitive markets by focusing on delivering value that larger competitors may overlook or need help to provide.

This highlights the importance of strategic clarity, operational excellence, and customer-centricity as key pillars for growth and long-term success in the marketplace.

Customer-Centric Business Models: A Case Study on Subway

In a rapidly evolving market where customer needs dictate success, businesses that focus solely on their products risk obsolescence. A prime example of this is the banking industry, where many institutions have lost significant customer bases due to their product-centric approaches. On the other hand, companies that place customers at the heart of their strategy, such as Subway, demonstrate how this shift can lead to remarkable success.

Subway: Revolutionizing the Fast-Food Industry

Subway, the global sandwich chain, provides a perfect case study of how customer-centricity can transform a business. Founded in 1965 by Fred DeLuca and his business partner, Dr. Peter Buck, the brand started with a small sandwich shop in Bridgeport, Connecticut. Fred DeLuca's primary goal was to fund his college education, but what set Subway apart was its commitment to giving customers control over their dining experience.

From its earliest days, Subway distinguished itself with its "build your own sandwich" model. Unlike other fast-food chains that offered pre-made meals, Subway allowed customers to select their preferred bread, meats, vegetables, and sauces, ensuring every meal was tailored to individual tastes and preferences. This emphasis on product customization was revolutionary and placed Subway at the forefront of customer-centric dining.

Key Elements of Subway's Customer-Centric Approach

1. **Product Customization:** Subway's core offering allowed customers to create their sandwiches exactly how they liked them. This level of personalization gave customers a sense of ownership over their meals, catering to a variety of dietary needs,

from vegetarian to gluten-free, which set them apart from competitors.
2. **Transparency in Food Preparation:** The chain's unique model of preparing food in front of customers built trust and created a more engaging experience. Customers could see the freshness of the ingredients and make real-time decisions about their orders, which strengthened the customer-brand connection.
3. **Customer Experience and Service:** Subway also placed a strong emphasis on providing friendly, attentive service. Staff were trained to offer personalized recommendations, further enhancing the customer's experience. This commitment to customer satisfaction extended beyond the meal itself, with initiatives like loyalty programs and special promotions designed to reward repeat customers.
4. **Leveraging Technology:** In recent years, Subway has embraced technology to further enhance the customer experience. Through mobile apps and self-service kiosks, customers can now place orders with greater convenience, selecting every ingredient digitally before arriving at the restaurant. These digital solutions streamline the ordering process and ensure accuracy, catering to the growing demand for efficiency and convenience.

The Impact of Subway's Customer-Centric Model

Subway's focus on the customer experience has had a profound impact on its success. By offering a customizable product and engaging customers at every touchpoint, Subway built a loyal customer base and expanded globally. Today, the brand operates over 40,000 locations across more than 100 countries.

Lessons for Other Businesses

Subway's journey underscores the importance of putting customers first. To replicate their success, businesses should:

- ✓ **Understand Their Audience:** Know who your customers are and what they want. Building a detailed buyer persona helps tailor products, services, and communications.
- ✓ **Map Customer Touchpoints:** Evaluate every interaction customers have with your brand and ensure it provides a seamless, satisfying experience.
- ✓ **Design for Customers:** Simplify processes and offer options that align with individual preferences, making your services more intuitive and enjoyable.
- ✓ **Foster a Customer-First Culture:** Empower employees to deliver exceptional service by prioritizing customer needs and feedback.
- ✓ **Continuously Improve:** Gather and act on customer feedback to enhance the experience over time, ensuring your brand evolves alongside customer expectations.

In conclusion, Subway's success is rooted in its ability to understand and cater to the evolving needs of its customers. By prioritizing the customer experience, the company has demonstrated that businesses can thrive in any industry by simply putting their customers at the center of their strategy.

Personalizing Customer Experiences:

The idea is to collect a diverse data set, which refers to a wide range of customer information, to make the user experience appealing. This data includes demographics, purchase history, browsing behavior, and more. By gathering such a comprehensive set of data, you can cater to different situations in the market, thereby appealing to various niches within a single market.

This method allows you to analyze behavioral data to create a seasonal promotion. The key idea here is to remember that the customers that you're trying to entice are human and that they would have interests outside the single market. This means that you can find a sense of expansion. Another way to have a personalized customer experience is through the Rolls Royce experience. Somewhere, you can personalize to appeal to the car's design to suit your preference. In a way, if you go to a shoemaker, he can make a shoe specifically for your needs compared to a readymade system.

The real benefit of personalizing the customer experience is the potential to enhance customer loyalty. When a customer perceives that a brand pays attention to every detail, even the seemingly unimportant ones, they develop a stronger affinity for the brand. This is further amplified when you identify and address a problem that your customer base shares but your competitors overlook. The ripple effect of a satisfied customer is powerful-they are more likely to recommend your brand to others, leading to a steady incline in your customer base.

The concept of personalized experiences yields great conversion rates because customers are more likely to invest in a product that is tailored to them. The key is to make your customers feel heard, to show them that their wants and needs are not just acknowledged but answered. When a company is perceived to do this, it is bound to succeed, as it fosters a sense of value and importance in the customer.

As elucidated through the example of Subway, these are some strategies to implement personalization in various business operations:

In today's business environment, while industries may share similarities, the unique dynamics of each enterprise must be carefully considered. Personalization has become a crucial factor in ensuring success, and it requires an understanding of not only the broader market but also the individual sensitivities of each business landscape. This means that to effectively implement personalized strategies, companies must recognize the specific context, challenges, and priorities of their customers.

Here are key strategies to integrate personalization into business operations:

1. **Understand the Customer's Environment:** The first step in personalization is a deep understanding of the customer's current environment. This includes recognizing what is most important to them at the time of engagement. Factors such as industry trends, regulatory pressures, and internal goals should be thoroughly researched. Personalization efforts must reflect the customer's unique challenges and goals. This insight enables businesses to offer solutions that feel tailor-made, building stronger connections and trust with customers.
2. **Thorough Market Research and Customer Insights:** Insisting on comprehensive research is essential before presenting any proposition. Collect data through surveys, feedback, and direct interactions to gain insights into your customers' behaviors, preferences, and pain points. Analyze this data to create detailed customer profiles or personas that guide how your business should interact with different segments. This ensures that your approach is relevant and resonates with the customer's immediate needs.
3. **Tailor-Made Solutions and Services:** Personalization isn't about offering generic solutions but about tailoring your product or service to meet specific customer demands. For instance, offering flexible product configurations, customized pricing plans, or specialized support can make your service stand out. Ensure that every recommendation or product feature is aligned with the customer's business goals and operational requirements, making your proposition a true solution rather than a one-size-fits-all offer.
4. **Real-Time Personalization:** In an increasingly digital world, businesses have the opportunity to offer real-time personalized experiences. Implementing tools like AI-driven recommendations, chatbots, and dynamic content delivery can provide customers with relevant information and solutions

exactly when they need them. This is particularly effective in e-commerce, software services, and customer support operations, where the ability to respond instantly to individual preferences can enhance the overall customer experience.

5. **Customer-Centric Communication:** Effective communication is at the heart of personalization. Engage with customers in ways that are meaningful and relevant to them. This could include personalized emails, industry-specific newsletters, or tailored offers based on past interactions. Businesses should avoid generic messaging, instead focusing on content that addresses the customer's specific needs and interests, helping them feel understood and valued.

6. **Position Your Proposition Based on Customer Priorities:** One of the key success factors in personalization is the ability to position your business offering in alignment with the customer's current priorities. This could mean emphasizing speed and efficiency for time-sensitive industries, cost-effectiveness for budget-conscious clients, or innovation for those seeking cutting-edge solutions. By clearly articulating how your business addresses their most pressing needs, you strengthen your value proposition.

Personalization is not a one-time activity. Regularly gathering feedback from customers and adapting your strategies accordingly contributes to a successful personalization experience. This could involve tweaking your offerings based on changing market conditions or adjusting communication styles to match new customer preferences. A commitment to ongoing personalization shows customers that you are invested in their long-term success.

Personalization in business operations is no longer a luxury but a necessity. By thoroughly understanding the customer landscape, aligning with their unique priorities, and adapting solutions to meet their specific needs, businesses can differentiate themselves in competitive markets. The companies that succeed in personalizing their operations are those that truly recognize the value of making their customers feel heard, understood, and appreciated.

The idea of exceeding customers comes from knowing your customer base; this idea is to learn all you can about what your customers want and need. There has to be a constant feedback loop to provide a sense of communication between the two sides of the market. The market consists not only of consumers but also of you. This is because the whole idea of the market is that one side needs to have a person providing the service, and another consumes the service. The idea is to maintain this momentum by constantly studying the preferences to make the product at the level of flagship quality.

Exceeding the customer's expectations will boost the customer's loyalty to you. Similar to personalizing, the customer will assume that you are listening to them or making a lot of effort to improve your product. This will give them more trust in your brand's system. This will also lead to a more supportive endorsement through word of mouth. This is always a good sign since you'll get a good inflow of new customers. Aside from that, it reflects well on the company. You don't normally hear positive feedback about a company that is failing.

In many cases, a customer's initial requirements are just the tip of the iceberg. Often, they may not fully communicate their needs or may be unaware of potential improvements to their current approach. Identifying these hidden opportunities not only allows businesses to meet expectations but also exceed them, creating stronger relationships and fostering loyalty. Here are some tips for identifying those opportunities to go above and beyond:

1. **Listen Actively and Ask Probing Questions:** While customers may outline their needs, it's important to dig deeper. Actively listen to their concerns and follow up with relevant questions to uncover underlying issues or additional pain points they may not

have expressed. Seeking feedback is pertinent, and this deeper understanding can reveal opportunities to provide more comprehensive solutions.
2. **Leverage Your Experience:** Drawing on your past experiences with similar projects or clients can help to identify potential problems before they arise. If you've encountered challenges in similar situations, use that knowledge to anticipate what your current customer may need next. Proactively offering suggestions based on your expertise not only showcases your value but also reassures customers that they are in capable hands.
3. **Be Empathetic and Solution-Oriented:** Empathy plays a key role in going above and beyond. Put yourself in the customer's shoes to understand their business pressures, goals, and constraints. This mindset will allow you to offer solutions that not only meet their needs but also make their lives easier. By offering thoughtful, solution-oriented advice, you demonstrate that you're genuinely invested in their success.
4. **Anticipate Future Needs:** Think beyond the immediate requirements. Consider the long-term implications of the customer's request and explore how your solution can scale with their future needs. Offering forward-thinking advice, such as scalability, upgrades, or additional features, ensures that your solution is adaptable, saving them time and resources down the line.
5. **Monitor Industry Trends and Innovations:** Stay informed about the latest trends, tools, and innovations in your customer's industry. By keeping ahead of the curve, you can offer suggestions that they may not have considered, giving you a competitive edge. Providing insights into new opportunities or potential risks they may face positions you as a strategic partner, not just a service provider.
6. **Identify Areas for Process Improvement:** Often, customers are so focused on the end result that they may overlook inefficiencies in their processes. Use your expertise to identify areas where operations could be streamlined, costs reduced, or

productivity improved. By offering these insights, you demonstrate that you're looking out for their best interests.
7. **Follow Up Regularly:** Going above and beyond doesn't end after delivering a solution. Regular follow-up with your customers to check if the solution is working as expected can provide insights into further improvements. This ongoing support strengthens trust and shows that you are committed to their long-term success.

By going beyond the surface and seeking out opportunities to improve your customer's experience, you create stronger relationships, build loyalty, and position yourself as a trusted partner. Empathy, proactive problem-solving, and leveraging your expertise are key to identifying ways to exceed customer expectations, leading to a deeper bond and lasting success.

Warning Against Complacency

It's crucial to stay agile and adaptive in the market to avoid becoming a forgotten entity. A prime example is Blockbuster, once the global leader in video retail. However, their failure to recognize the potential of online streaming allowed competitors like Netflix to surpass them, relegating Blockbuster to a mere memory in the market.

This drawback is massive in the eyes of the market because it leaves a bad impression on your company. You are more likely to carry this image even if you somehow make a comeback. You will make an impression on the customers that you are not always at the ship's helm. This means that you will be considered a brand that does not provide decent customer service, if any.

The idea is that the company is just out to profit from nostalgia and that your product is a novelty. This was the case with Nokia when it came back to the market. People thought it was just a phone company that would play the imitation game. However, they found a way around partnering with Microsoft to make the 'Lumia.' This, however, backfired on the Microsoft OS and the Nokia company since the bad image made it so that the device was not given a chance to express its potential. After this, Nokia was left to fade back into history. The company is back on the market. However, they are still running the tactile keypad phones of the old days, solidifying themselves as a phone company that caters to the elderly.

Maintaining a market position is difficult when you fall behind in innovation. A company may not make a return; if it does, it has to play the catch-up race. Microsoft is making an OS for mobile phones and other handheld devices. The issue here is not just that Google and Apple have had a head start with their OSs; the problem is that they have a strong hold on the market, in the sense that some features intend to brandish their differences or boast their superiority. Google's Android, on the one hand, has taken the Microsoft Windows approach of providing its OS to any company that needs it. After this campaign, they built their line of mobile phones, whereas Apple has had their OS perform on their line of products. It has been the tradition at Apple to keep their secrets to themselves, but with these two being neck and neck, there is no room for any more faces to enter this conflict.

Building Customer Relationships:

The idea is to establish a strong bond with your customer base and build on their confidence in your service. This is essential since you must know that the customer is what you have when creating your image. You could be isolated from your core audience if they are alienated from the service or brand. The idea is to enhance the customer's lifetime value, which means you must provide a lasting service. An example of this is the Superdry clothing brand. They offer a good product with high-end materials and fine attention to detail regarding tailoring. This makes the customers think that though expensive, they will provide a sustainable product. This keeps the customers coming in for more. To add to this is the idea of versatility. It helps with the brand image since you can use the product multiple times, making it more appealing to the customers.

Another way to maintain a good rapport is to respond positively to feedback. There are cases of companies not responding to genuinely helpful feedback. That has led customers to file petitions to rectify the problem. This is something that no customer wants to deal with; this happens more with companies that have grown too big for their own good. There was a case with Apple where they did not intend to update their chargers with Type C cables like every other device. This made it difficult for the users, yet there was no resolution. The issue was resolved when the EU got involved. This shows a model not to follow since, as a company, you would be just starting. At this point, no company has developed a cult-like following like Apple.

On delivering exceptional value, it's crucial to sum up everything—from forming the right team to identifying business gaps and creating a unique value proposition. Effective resource optimization ensures we build and deliver persuasively to customers, maintaining strong communication and measurable goals. In system integration, our success hinges on competency across multiple technologies and certified resources, coupled with robust program management skills. Researching client landscapes deeply and adding our unique value proposition solidifies our position even against global giants. Our ability to manage large-scale implementations globally underscores our commitment to exceeding expectations. Customer feedback and vendor audits consistently rank us ahead, highlighting our meticulous attention to detail and commitment to exceptional service.

Reflecting on another client's case, where a competitor folded, leaving their solution unsupported, we swiftly ensured continued support and began planning migration solutions. By demonstrating proactive support and exceeding immediate needs, we reinforced our commitment to customer success and gained their trust in navigating future challenges. Going above and beyond to solve immediate problems is key to positioning ourselves as trusted partners in the market.

Gaining Trust Through Authentic Feedback:

The idea is to maintain a positive feedback loop, initiating a Reddit community, a platform widely used by gaming enthusiasts, where you can see different members talk about the services you've provided them. In this way, you can learn how to improve the services. Also, you can reply to major problems with troubleshooting hints to guide your audience to an easy fix. Many gaming companies are doing this to improve the user experience, making the fanbases more loyal to the game than to abandon it. This also shows that the developers are also human and can make mistakes.

With a more communicative approach, you also develop a competitive edge. Because you know what the customers want before many of your competitors, this means that for your niche, you will be leading the charge by being the first to address and resolve customer issues while the others are playing the imitation game.

You, on the lead, could spell many upsides to this since you can fashion the market to your liking. However, this also means that many of the competition will have their eye on you, leading to potential sabotaging attempts. This could manifest as a counter-advertising attack, as Pepsi and Coca-Cola have done in the international market. If you are on your toes replying to the customer base, you can stand your ground. Additionally, your customers will still support your campaign because you are a responsive party regarding customer support. You're in a good position if you have a good rapport with your customer base. Plus, you can expand into markets beyond your current position, which could lead to you having a stronger data pool. This could help you make bigger strides as you know what to improve regarding your product.

You can do good work as long as your core users are strong. This is because you have the support of those loyal to your brand who will hold out on your behalf. This is similar to users who enjoyed the experience of playing with LEGOs as children. The LEGO community got together to save the company when it ran out of funds, demonstrating the power of customer loyalty. This happened with the advent of video games and a bigger push from other toy manufacturers. This made the company fall out of favor in the market. However, the community banded together and revived the company. After this, they started partnering with other franchises to make the company more appealing to newer customers. They still appeased the customer base by reintroducing the older sets with a nostalgia theme.

Strategies for Delivering Exceptional Value: Insights from System Integration and Global Competition

Delivering Exceptional Value to Customers

In discussing the strategy for delivering exceptional value, I would like to emphasize that success hinges on several critical factors. First, it's essential to assemble the right team and identify gaps in the market to craft a unique value proposition. Second, optimizing resources and maintaining effective communication is vital for aligning with customer goals that truly matter at the time.

System Integration Challenges and Strategies

Competence across multiple technologies and domains is paramount in system integration, particularly when dealing with fragmented ecosystems and global clientele. Resource certification ensures the capability to provide tailored solutions. Robust program management is crucial and indispensable for overseeing large-scale implementations across diverse geographies and time zones.

Success Against Global Competition

Highlighting a pivotal success story, the discussion turned to overcoming formidable global competition in a major enterprise migration project. The keys to triumph included meticulous client research, enabling a deep understanding of client needs, and meticulous program management skills. These elements, combined with a compelling, unique value proposition, underscored the company's ability to compete and excel beyond established industry giants.

Consistent Value Delivery

Meticulous planning and execution are fundamental to our ability to consistently deliver exceptional value. Our track record in customer audits, where we consistently outpace competitors, demonstrates our capability to meet and exceed client expectations. This reinforces the importance of detailed planning, effective program management, and a strong, unique value proposition in creating a distinct position in competitive markets, ultimately fostering long-term client loyalty and satisfaction.

At *Fidrox*, we're not just delivering value—we're doing it in a way that stands apart. As a niche player, we possess a unique skill set that is particularly effective in addressing critical aspects of your solution, where customers often struggle to find a suitable vendor. Our distinctiveness in this area becomes a significant value-add as we solve problems no one else can, which inevitably shines a spotlight on us, even in the presence of larger competitors.

For example, customers have been thrilled with our ability to resolve issues that, while not seemingly significant, are critical because there's no one else to address them. This has allowed us to steal the limelight, earning recognition despite the presence of bigger players. Our approach creates a perception of expertise and trust among customers, helping us carve out our space in their operations.

As we expand beyond our niche offerings, it's crucial to maintain strategic planning and deliver exceptional outcomes, especially when competing with incumbents. While we've succeeded in capturing parts of their market, our strategy must continue to emphasize differentiation to sustain the value we bring.

In my experience, our startup operated in a crowded ecosystem with numerous subsystems. Our niche was integrating these subsystems, making the customer's job easier and aligning with their enterprise workflows—an unmet need in the market. Starting with this niche, we eventually expanded to take over the entire ecosystem solution. This large-scale implementation was intentional, as we aimed to work exclusively with large enterprises, ensuring greater value for the time and effort invested. Rather than pursuing numerous small and medium-sized enterprises (SMEs), we chose to focus on a single large client that would provide depth, breadth, and a strong reference for future business. Large enterprises also have more compelling needs, such as automation or audit compliance, which aren't as pressing for SMEs.

Beyond our technical expertise and certifications, we knew that large program management skills were essential when working with such enterprises. This is particularly true when dealing with multiple geographies, time zones, and countries. We couldn't afford mistakes, so we invested in robust program management capabilities with extensive templates and systems to manage large-scale implementations. This level of planning was vital to instilling confidence in our customers, especially those who were initially apprehensive about working with a small company. While we came from large enterprise backgrounds, our startup demonstrated that we could handle complex, large-scale projects.

Despite any initial concerns, we exceeded expectations by not just meeting basic requirements but delivering far beyond what was anticipated. This approach left a lasting, positive impression. Today, we are a nine-year-old company, and many of the customers who started with us remain with us. We've grown stronger each year and have become their de facto consultant and implementation partner. By carefully observing market needs and aligning our offerings with the requirements of enterprise customers, we have positioned ourselves to develop all the possibilities within this landscape.

So, this approach becomes a foundation for me to conceive new ideas, revisit the customer, and show them how implementing these ideas can benefit them. If they express interest, we build the solutions, demonstrate how they work, and, if successful, offer them as a formal solution. This not only strengthens our relationship with that customer but also opens the door to offering similar solutions to others. In this way, the landscape becomes a testing ground where I can experiment and innovate, which is crucial in business growth.

For a small company like ours, every detail must be meticulously planned, as there is no room for error. If the customer loses confidence, it's incredibly difficult to regain. That's why servicing them well is vital, especially in the early stages. As a small startup, we must pay close attention to the specifics and provide a level of service they won't receive from larger organizations. For those larger firms, the customer may just be one among many, but for us, they are the customer, deserving of all our focus and effort.

Of course, scaling the business presents its own challenges. As you grow, it becomes harder to maintain that same level of attention, and eventually, you may view them as just another customer.

However, by the time you reach that stage, you'll have established yourself in the market. That's why it makes sense to use the startup's small size to your advantage, leveraging your ability to plan, adapt, and deliver exceptional value, because this builds the foundation for future growth. Providing exceptional value at this stage will go a long way towards expanding your customer base and creating new opportunities with your existing clients.

In fact, today, we've achieved things that even our multinational competitors cannot match. Thanks to our ability to deeply understand and address customer needs, we've been the first to offer certain solutions on a global scale. This level of customer trust is invaluable.

They now turn to us with confidence, knowing we can deliver on requirements no one else can. That's the result of our dedication to doing things right and ensuring we don't make mistakes.

It's equally important to know your limits. If you're not confident about a particular challenge, don't take it on and risk undermining the trust you've built. Shaking a customer's confidence is hard to recover from.

Instead, focus on what you do best and continually refine those processes to ensure that what you promise is delivered to the highest standard. Regular communication with the customer—through periodic meetings to update them on progress—goes a long way in reinforcing trust and satisfaction.

In my experience, this approach has had long-lasting benefits. I've seen people move to new companies and bring us with them simply because of the unique value we provided in their previous roles. What you invest in initially—time, effort, and a commitment to exceeding expectations—pays dividends in the long run.

Attracting new customers is closely tied to your ability to solve problems effectively, but it's not just about solving them; it's about exceeding expectations. This requires careful planning and strategic delivery. By doing this consistently, you can build strong, loyal relationships with your clients.

Consistency and strategic persuasion are key—these are not just business buzzwords but principles that lead to success. In my experience, these elements have been critical in delivering sustained value to our customers, helping us grow and thrive in a competitive landscape.

To sum up my experience in terms of delivering value to our customers:

- Understanding and anticipating customer needs is foundational to delivering value.
- Personalization enhances customer experiences and satisfaction.
- Consistently exceeding expectations differentiates your business and fosters loyalty.
- Continuous improvement in value delivery is crucial to stay relevant and competitive.
- Authentic engagement and feedback are key to understanding and meeting customer needs better.

Here's your call for action: Identify one way your business can go beyond meeting to exceeding customer expectations this week. Implement it, gather feedback, and refine your approach based on what you learn. Remember, delivering exceptional value is an ongoing journey of understanding, anticipation, and adaptation.

Having laid the groundwork for delivering exceptional value to your customers, you're now poised to weave these principles into every aspect of your business. As we transition to the conclusion of this book, let's reflect on the journey we've undertaken and how the principles of value-driven entrepreneurship can propel us toward achieving our goals and creating meaningful impact in our businesses and communities.

CONCLUSION

As we come to the close of this book, I hope you've gained more than just practical strategies for entrepreneurship. I hope you've found a renewed sense of purpose, clarity, and—most importantly—an understanding of your own identity. The journey of entrepreneurship, as we've explored, is not only about building something external but about the process of becoming, evolving, and uncovering who we truly are.

Throughout this book, we have explored the foundations of a value-driven business: breaking through fear, crafting a vision aligned with your core values, building resilience, and delivering exceptional value to others. But at its heart, this book is about you and the transformation that occurs when you pursue entrepreneurship as a path to self-discovery.

The journey doesn't end here. Entrepreneurship, like any worthwhile pursuit, is a continuous process of growth. As you move forward, remember the insights and lessons you've gathered on these pages. When you face challenges, let them reveal new layers of your character. When you reach success, let them remind you of your purpose. Let your business be an extension of who you are and a means to make a meaningful impact on the world.

Thank you for allowing me to join you on this journey. My hope is that you will continue in pursuit of your own identity, forging a path that is uniquely yours. Remember that your greatest achievement isn't just in what you create but in who you become along the way.

Here's to the journey ahead, one that I hope brings you closer to your true self.

— RAJ GOPAL

www.ingramcontent.com/pod-product-compliance
Lightning Source LLC
Chambersburg PA
CBHW021008090426
42738CB00007B/710